MACMILLAN MODERN NOVELISTS

IRIS MURDOCH

Hilda D. Spear

MACMILLAN

First published 1995 by
MACMILLAN PRESS LTD
Houndmills, Basingstoke, Hampshire RG21 2XS
and London
Companies and representatives
throughout the world

ISBN 0–333–51923–X hardcover
ISBN 0–333–51924–8 paperback

A catalogue record for this book is available
from the British Library.

10   9   8   7   6   5   4   3   2   1
04   03   02   01   00   99   98   97   96   95

Printed in Malaysia

Series Standing Order (Macmillan Modern Novelists)

If you would like to receive future titles in this series as they are
published, you can make use of our standing order facility. To place a
standing order please contact your bookseller, or, in case of difficulty,
write to us at the address below with your name and address and the
name of the series. Please state with which title you wish to begin your
standing order. (If you live outside the United Kingdom we may not
have the rights for your area, in which case we will forward your order
to the publisher concerned.)

Customer Services Department, Macmillan Distribution Ltd
Houndmills, Basingstoke, Hampshire, RG21 2XS, England.

MACMI

MACMILLAN MODERN NOVELISTS

To Walter, Gillian, Kathryn and little Jasmin

Contents

Acknowledgements

I should like to thank my husband Walter Spear for reading through the draft and making comments and corrections. I am also grateful to John Bayley for reading through an early draft of Chapter 1 and to both him and Iris Murdoch for their cooperation and kindness. Thanks are also due for help in various ways to Helmut Bonheim, to Alan Grant of Dundee University Library and to my students at Dundee University who took the Post-War British Fiction course with me.

The author and publishers are grateful to Iris Murdoch for permission to reproduce extracts from the following works: *Under the Net*, *The Flight from the Enchanter*, *The Sandcastle*, *The Bell*, *A Severed Head*, *An Unofficial Rose*, *The Unicorn*, *The Italian Girl*, *The Red and the Green*, *The Time of the Angels*, *The Nice and the Good*, *Bruno's Dream*, *A Fairly Honourable Defeat*, *The Black Prince*, *A Word Child*, *Henry and Cato*, *The Sea, The Sea*, *Nuns and Soldiers*, *The Philosopher's Pupil*, *The Good Apprentice*, *The Message to the Planet*, *The Green Knight*, *Sartre: Romantic Rationalist*, 'Against Dryness', *The Sovereignty of Good*, *The Fire and the Sun*, *A Year of Birds*, *The Servants and the Snow* and *Metaphysics as a Guide to Morals*; and to A. S. Byatt for permission to reproduce extracts from *Degrees of Freedom* and from *The Shadow of the Sun*.

General Editor's Preface

The death of the novel has often been announced, and part of the secret of its obstinate vitality must be its capacity for growth, adaptation, self-renewal and self-transformation: like some vigorous organism in a speeded-up Darwinian ecosystem, it adapts itself quickly to a changing world. War and revolution, economic crisis and social change, radically new ideologies such as Marxism and Freudianism, have made this century unprecedented in human history in the speed and extent of change, but the novel has shown an extraordinary capacity to find new forms and techniques and to accommodate new ideas and conceptions of human nature and human experience, and even to take up new positions on the nature of fiction itself.

In the generations immediately preceding and following 1914, the novel underwent a radical redefinition of its nature and possibilities. The present series of monographs is devoted to the novelists who created the modern novel and to those who, in their turn, either continued and extended, or reacted against and rejected, the traditions established during that period of intense exploration and experiment. It includes a number of those who lived and wrote in the nineteenth century but whose innovative contribution to the art of fiction makes it impossible to ignore them in any account of the origins of the modern novel; it also includes the so-called 'modernists' and those who in the mid- and late twentieth century have emerged as outstanding practitioners of this genre. The scope is, inevitably, international; not only, in the migratory and exile-haunted

world of our century, do writers refuse to heed national frontiers –
'English' literature lays claim to Conrad the Pole, Henry James the
American, and Joyce the Irishman – but geniuses such as Flaubert,
Dostoevsky and Kafka have had an influence on the fiction of many
nations.

Each volume in the series is intended to provide an introduction
to the fiction of the writer concerned, both for those approaching
him or her for the first time and for those who are already familiar
with some parts of the achievement in question and now wish to
place it in the context of the total *œuvre*. Although essential information relating to the writer's life and times is given, usually in an
opening chapter, the approach is primarily critical and the emphasis
is not upon 'background' or generalisations but upon close examination of important texts. Where an author is notably prolific, major texts have been made to convey, more summarily, a sense of
the nature and quality of the author's work as a whole. Those who
want to read further will find suggestions in the select bibliography
included in each volume. Many novelists are, of course, not only
novelists but also poets, essayists, biographers, dramatists, travel
writers and so forth; many have practised shorter forms of fiction;
and many have written letters or kept diaries that constitute a significant part of their literary output. A brief study cannot hope to
deal with all these in detail, but where the shorter fiction and the
non-fictional writings, public and private, have an important relationship to the novels, some space has been devoted to them.

NORMAN PAGE

List of Abbreviations

ASH	A Severed Head
AUR	An Unofficial Rose
BD	Bruno's Dream
BP	The Black Prince
DOF	Degrees of Freedom
FAS	The Fire and the Sun
FE	The Flight from the Enchanter
FHD	A Fairly Honourable Defeat
GA	The Good Apprentice
GK	The Green Knight
HC	Henry and Cato
MGM	Metaphysics as a Guide to Morals
MTTP	The Message to the Planet
NS	Nuns and Soldiers
PP	The Philosopher's Pupil
SOG	The Sovereignty of Good
SRR	Sartre: Romantic Rationalist
The Sea	The Sea, The Sea
TIG	The Italian Girl
TNTG	The Nice and the Good
TOA	The Time of the Angels
TRATG	The Red and the Green
TS	The Sandcastle
TU	The Unicorn
UTN	Under the Net

1
Introduction

In the twenty-five novels she has published since 1954,[1] Iris Murdoch has avoided what she sees as 'the obvious danger for a writer' – writing autobiographical novels. The settings may well reflect backgrounds familiar to her, and the civil servants, university dons and Irish characters may seem to belong to the milieu of her own life, but the narrative, the plots, the bizarre relationships are creations of her lively imagination. We must not expect to find in her novels accounts of her own life and she herself is on record as saying that she believes that she as author should not be in her books. To that extent, then, she follows the dictates of modernism. Like most novelists, however, she identifies with a wide range of her characters, but they are not individual people she has known in life, though she has known some of her dog characters. Nevertheless, as will be seen, her *experience* of life is frequently incorporated into her novels. This is especially apparent in the London settings of the majority of her novels, for she displays simultaneously the detailed and intimate knowledge of the metropolis that only a long acquaintance during childhood and particularly later in her early working life could have given her, and the slightly blasé attitude, though not the contempt that familiarity is supposed to breed. Likewise, such aspects of her personality as her friendships with dogs, her obsessive love of the sea, or her interest in stones – to see, to feel and to collect them – creep into several of the novels.

Iris Murdoch was born in Dublin on 15 July 1919, the only child of an Anglo-Irish mother and an Irish or Scots-Irish father; though,

1

despite her mixed national background, she states at times that both her parents were Irish. As she suggests, however, the statements are not contradictory:

> my Irishness is Anglo-Irishness in a very strict sense. I think this is a very special way of being Irish. . . . I'm profoundly Irish and I've been conscious of this all my life . . .[2]

Her bright and cheerful mother had been training as an opera singer when she married at the age of eighteen and gave up her intended career to dedicate herself to her husband and home. From her mother Murdoch seems to have inherited her artistic interests and her sense of humour as well as a pleasant and attractive singing voice; from her more serious father she inherited her intellectual ability and interest. When she was a year old, the family left Ireland and moved to London where her father joined the Civil Service. Since her childhood was spent mainly in London, she was deprived of any extended family, for her Irish relations were far away and, though she often spent holidays in Ireland, the day-to-day intimacy of close-knit relationships did not feature in her upbringing. In an interview with John Haffenden in 1983 she remarked that she was able to identify with exiles because she herself is 'a kind of exile, a displaced person'.[3]

Like so many only children, she used to think that she would like to have a brother and her novels are full of sibling relationships, often stiflingly close; twins seem to have a special attraction for her, particularly twins of different sexes; she delights, too, in half-relationships which allow her characters to have an extra parent or so and thus confuse their origins. As she grew older, however, she gradually came to the conclusion that a brother might well have had an adverse effect upon her own life for he might have had all the money available for education and she would have missed the opportunity of going to Oxford. To some extent a feminist *cause célèbre* was thus denied her for, brotherless, she was deprived of nothing in her early life in favour of it being bestowed on a male counterpart. Unlike many of her female contemporaries, therefore, she has had no external compulsions upon her to espouse the cause of feminism and has responded to life and experience without the burden of 'gender-consciousness' being thrust upon her. As a result it would be difficult to find in her work specifically female subject matter; though the patriarchal world which she presents is fairly traditional, however, in its treatment of men and women, it is clear that, as an author, she is very conscious of the unfairness of a world in which a married woman is just 'a subdivision of her husband's mind' (BP, p. 176).

As it was, Murdoch herself was able to have her parents' undivided attention and there was no need to share their love with brothers or sisters; they were a very close-knit family and she spent an extremely happy childhood. Despite this, when she depicts children in her novels they frequently seem to be at odds with their parents. For instance, in *The Sandcastle*, when children are first introduced, they are a cause for dissension between their schoolteacher father and their mother. In the later novel, *An Unofficial Rose*, the scheming, mischief-making and rather objectionable Miranda is instrumental in ruining her mother's life, and David Gavender in *The Sacred and Profane Love Machine*, perhaps more understandably, is unable to forgive his father for deserting his mother and himself. On the other hand, the twins, Edward and Henrietta in *The Nice and the Good,* are likeable enough, even though they can hardly be seen as quite ordinary children. Many of the later novels, from *A Word Child* onward are mainly childless, or at least deal with adolescents, or children who are moving towards adolescence as the story proceeds, though the small boy Adam and his dog Zed play a not-altogether-insignificant part in *The Philosopher's Pupil* and Irina in *The Message to the Planet* is still a child when we first meet her. The most recent novel, *The Green Knight*, however, places a group of adolescents, the youngest fifteen, the oldest nineteen – not exactly children, but by no means mature adults – somewhere near its centre.

Murdoch's interest in stories began in childhood with Lewis Carroll's 'Alice books', with *Kim* and with *Treasure Island*, books which fired her imagination and provided her with the excitement and the magic necessary for stimulating her creative faculties. She explains that her father encouraged her to read and to read widely, both children's books and those for grown-ups. It was an excellent preparation for her later creative and academic interests.

She began her formal education at day-school, attending a Froebel Institute near her home in London. After this, her education may be

seen as conforming to the conventional and traditional pattern of
the middle and upper-middle classes at the time. Despite the loving
family background, in 1931 when she was twelve years old, she
was sent away to be a boarder at Badminton School in Bristol where
she was at first extremely homesick. It was perhaps the memory of
this period in her life that helped to make Penn's homesickness in
An Unofficial Rose a felt misery. Murdoch trusted her parents' judgement about her education, however, and settled down. She grew to
enjoy school and it was there that she developed her interest in
classics, in modern languages and in literature.

In 1938 she left her single-sex public school to go to a women's
college, Somerville, at Oxford; it was more common than not in
those days for girls to receive the whole of their education among
their own sex, though at Oxford at least there was inevitably some
mixing with the male undergraduates. At Somerville Murdoch read
'Greats' (classics, philosophy and ancient history), gaining a First
in her B.A. examinations in 1942. Even her membership of the
Communist Party during her undergraduate days may be seen as
rather conventional; Marxism flourished in the universities at that
time, particularly in Oxbridge, and it was a common enough phenomenon, especially among the more high-minded students, to become
members of 'the Party'. For Murdoch, as for so many others, it
represented a rebellion against her upbringing and her background.
Likewise, her subsequent disillusion with Marxist ideals followed
what had become a quite predictable course.

During her years at university she displayed a rare capacity to
endear herself to fellow-students of both sexes. At this time she
was described by her university contemporaries as being of a 'stun-
ning' beauty and photographs from round about that time confirm
this. These years were marred, however, by the advent of war in
September 1939. At that time many young men who would have
gone to the university left school and went straight into the Forces
and many others found their university courses interrupted by their
enlistment or conscription. Sadly, Murdoch's first emotional involvement, with fellow Oxford student Frank Thompson, ended with his
tragic wartime death when, in June 1944, he was shot as a spy in
occupied Bulgaria. Like so many young men he had joined up at
the outbreak of war and served in both Turkey and the Middle East
before being sent to Macedonia to try to find out about German

troop movements. Following his capture he was imprisoned, 'tried' and sentenced to death. Over thirty years later Murdoch wrote of him in a letter to *The Times* that he was:

> a poet, a person of exceptional charm and sweetness, always full of jokes and fun, a lover of art and of nature, a scholar, a man of the highest principles, delicate, scrupulous and tender.[4]

After completing her own degree at Oxford, Iris Murdoch herself went straight into the Civil Service as an Assistant Principal in the Treasury, living and working in wartime London. When the war ended, however, she felt the need to do some social work to help those who had been displaced and disorientated in the conflict, so she went to work for the United Nations Relief and Rehabilitation Administration, (UNRRA) first as an organiser in London and then travelling to Belgium and Austria, working in displaced persons' camps; it was simply, she comments, 'a question of feeding people', though there is little doubt that during this time she came face to face with many of the horrors and cruelties that man inflicts upon man.

Her experiences with UNRRA left an indelible impression on her mind and emphasised her identification with exiles; throughout her novels there are depictions of exiles and refugees, illegal immigrants who have fled the horrors of their own country, men and women trying to escape from their past. Yet they are not always sympathetically portrayed; the Lusiewicz brothers in *The Flight from the Enchanter* have minds which appear to be permanently distorted by their early experiences, whilst Julius King in *A Fairly Honourable Defeat* has brought the evils of Belsen back to Britain from the prison camp and he destroys the innocent and essentially good Rupert out of sheer pride and malice. On the other hand, the gentle Eugene Peshkov from *The Time of the Angels* is pure goodness and Willy Kost in *The Nice and the Good*, though irreparably damaged by his experiences in Dachau, lives without malice.

Though Murdoch enjoyed reading literature at school, her university studies concentrated her interests in philosophy and the classics and her first publications in the early 1950s concerned themselves with philosophical matters – metaphysics and existentialism. Thus, after her stint with UNRRA she applied for and was awarded a scholarship to go to the USA in order to further her philosophical

studies. It was not to be, for, though she was no longer a member
of the Communist Party, she was refused a visa on account of her
previous membership; thus, despite her anger against the decision,
she remained in Britain. What had at the time seemed harsh perhaps changed the course of her life and saved her for us as a dis-
tinctly English novelist. In 1947, after a period of reading and thinking
and helped by a Sarah Smithson Studentship in Philosophy, she
decided to return to academic life and spent a year at Newnham
College, Cambridge, before returning to Oxford in 1948 as lecturer
in Philosophy and Fellow of St Anne's College. By this time, she
knew that she 'wanted to teach philosophy, wanted to be a writer
and wanted to be in Oxford'. That same year, four years after Frank
Thompson's death, she met Franz Steiner, a Czechoslovakian Jew
whose parents had been deported and killed by the Nazis; there was
an immediate and mutual attraction between them. Trained as an
anthropologist, Steiner was also a poet and despite the horror of his
life, Iris Murdoch described him as a 'delightful, funny, clever, charm-
ing creature'. When they met in 1948 Steiner was already a sick
man and the following year he had a heart attack but he struggled
on for another three years before his death in 1952.

By now Murdoch was writing novels. She wrote several before
she was satisfied enough to send one to a publisher but even then it
was rejected and she subsequently destroyed it, together with the
other early ones; *Under the Net*, however, was accepted by Chatto
& Windus, the first publisher she approached with it, and was published in 1954. The satisfying association between author and publisher has continued until the present day. Two years later she married
the critic and scholar John Bayley, to whom she dedicated *The
Sandcastle* which was then in gestation and which was published
the following year. Twenty years later she was to dedicate *The Fire
and the Sun* (1977) to him as well. Bayley, too, is a novelist, though
with a more slender output; he followed a busy academic career,
finally retiring from the Warton Professorship of English Literature
in Oxford in 1992. It has been a happy and supportive marriage,
enabling Murdoch to write in peace and security. An eccentric and
knowledgeable cook, John Bayley prepares the meals and his influence in this line may be seen in the interest in food and cooking
that frequently surfaces in the novels, particularly, perhaps, in *The
Sea, The Sea*; he is, too, a well-informed polymath and Murdoch

at times turns to him for assistance in technical matters, especially anything to do with firearms, but in general she does not discuss her novels with him until they are complete. Murdoch's work shows immense industry; her twenty-fifth and most recent novel, *The Green Knight*, was published in 1993, thirty-nine years after the first – an average of one novel every eighteen months, to say nothing of the philosophical books which have been slotted in at times between the fictional works.

The last fifteen years or so have brought Iris Murdoch both national and international recognition; not only has she been awarded a number of prestigious literary prizes, including the Booker Prize for *The Sea, The Sea* in 1978, but she has also been admitted to the Irish Academy, the American Academy of Arts and Letters and the American Academy of Sciences. She is a Fellow of St Anne's College, Oxford, and has been given an Honorary D.Litt. from the University of Oxford. Furthermore, in 1987, following a CBE awarded in 1976, she was honoured with a DBE. That same year she was distinguished with a rare honour for a living novelist by having her portrait (painted by Tom Phillips) hung in the National Portrait Gallery.

This bare outline of her life gives little sense of the personality that lies behind it and, indeed, Murdoch has constantly protected her own privacy so that biographical facts are not easy to come by.

Whilst she was philosophy tutor at St Anne's, Murdoch was busily following two careers, teaching and writing about philosophy and simultaneously writing her novels. M. Bernard Le Gros has seen this duality as 'the central problem which Iris Murdoch's work poses for us' and he goes on to ask:

> is she a novelist-philosopher or a novelist *and* a philosopher? In other words, is there a relationship between her novels and her philosophy and if so, what is this relationship? (*Rencontres*, p. 63, my translation).

The problem must continue to be kept under review, for Murdoch's interest in philosophy has been maintained throughout her career; the names and ideas of philosophers, particularly of Sartre and Plato, frequently crop up in her novels and many of her characters indulge in philosophical discussions, though not necessarily on the level of academic philosophy. There is, it would seem, a difference between a 'philosophical novel' and a novel which is concerned with modes of thought which may be seen as philosophical. As early as March 1950 Murdoch published two philosophical articles in *The Listener* and she has continued to publish articles and books on philosophy at intervals ever since, though she is somewhat dismissive of the suggestion that she herself is a philosopher. In answer to M. Le Gros she remarks:

> I am a teacher of philosophy and I am trained as a philosopher and I 'do' philosophy and I teach philosophy, but philosophy is fantastically difficult and I think those who attempt to write it would probably agree that there are very few moments when they rise to the level of real philosophy. One is writing about philosophy . . . One is not actually doing the real thing. (*Rencontres*, p. 79).

Her first book, published in 1953, the year before *Under the Net*, was *Sartre: Romantic Rationalist,* and, being about Sartre rather than about pure philosophical concepts, it seems to illustrate her statement; she is writing about Sartre and his theories; she is not postulating new and original philosophic theories of her own. It is perhaps very much a pointer to her underlying interests at the time that the book, although essentially a philosophical study, is based on a consideration of Sartre's novels which, she suggests, 'provide more comprehensive material for a study of his thought' (*SRR*, p. 138). In 1945, during the time she was working for UNRRA she met Sartre, albeit briefly, and he was an early influence upon her, though the book itself does not suggest discipleship and by the time it was published she was clearly not in tune with his philosophic thought. Her main disagreement with him lies in his treatment of human relationships; as she explains:

> It is on the lonely awareness of the individual and not on the individual's integration with his society that his attention centres. In Sartre's world rational awareness is in inverse ratio to social integration (*SRR*, p. 62).

It is a point we have to return to when we consider Murdoch's own novels for, at least theoretically, she sees the contingent as integral

to life; 'the world is contingent and infinitely various', she comments in her introduction to the 1987 edition of the book (*SRR*,
p. 38); it thus follows that the isolated individual is completely at
odds with his society and can be a representation of no one but
himself.

In her first novel, *Under The Net*, which followed hard on the
heels of *Sartre, Romantic Rationalist*, the solipsistic narrator, Jake
'hate[s] contingency' (*UTN*, p. 24); by the end of the plot he is
brought to understand that society does not revolve around him but
rather that he is part of a highly complex human world. The essay,
'Against Dryness',[5] was written a few years later and was in gestation at the same time as her husband's influential book, *The Characters of Love* (1960). The two publications are united in their
emphasis on the need for the novelist to depict 'real' characters and
in their rejection of the primacy of the 'author's consciousness'. At
the end of her article Murdoch returns to a brief discussion of Sartre's
ideas and she ends her argument with a consideration of 'truth' in
literature: 'Real people are destructive of myth, contingency is destructive of fantasy and opens the way for imagination' (Bradbury,
p. 31). The theme of fantasy versus imagination is a recurrent one
in her non-fiction and is a significant index to an understanding of
her fiction. As we investigate the novels more closely we shall find
that, though the surface level of many of them appears to have
mythological significance, at a deeper level there are real people
suffering real human emotions and the apparent superficiality of
the plot is subverted by what turns out to be an imaginative presentation of reality. She sees herself as a 'realistic writer' and as one
who wants to write about life, as 'life is very terrible and very
funny'.

In the discussions of her work which took place in Caen and
were later published as *Rencontres avec Iris Murdoch* she commented
that even when she wrote *Sartre, Romantic Rationalist* she did not
entirely agree with Sartre's ideas and she now feels 'very far away
from him' (*Rencontres*, p. 78). In the same discussion, in answer to
a question, she suggested a kind of 'course' of reading for a non-
philosopher who wished to move towards a philosophical way of
thinking; her proposals, put forward tentatively and with many quali-
fications, included Plato's *Symposium*, John Stuart Mill's *Utilitarian-
ism*, Kant's *The Fundamental Principles of the Metaphysics of Morals*,

Sartre's *Existentialisme et Humanisme*, 'some Berkeley . . . of course
Descartes . . . Merleau-Ponty . . . David Hume . . . Hegel' (*Rencontres*,
pp. 79–80). Such a catholic choice, brought out on the spur of the
moment, is daunting and probably still leaves the uninitiated in a
state of uncertainty. We might observe, however, that in order of
priority her mind turned first to Plato.

Her later philosophical books, the book of essays, *The Sovereignty of Good* (1970), the Romanes lectures published in 1977 as
The Fire and the Sun: Why Plato Banished the Artists and her Platonic imitation, *Acastos: Two Platonic Dialogues* (1986) suggest where
her fundamental philosophical interests lie and illustrate her movement away from Sartrean Existentialism in the thirty and more years
since she published her first book. To some extent she has reacted
against Sartre's early influence and, in a talk she gave at Dundee
University in 1983 she described Plato as 'the most satisfying philosopher'. Certainly it is with Plato that she has been most concerned in her philosophical writings, though she rejects many of his
views on Art: 'Plato never did justice to the unique truth-conveying
capacities of art', she comments in *The Fire and the Sun* (p. 85).
Nevertheless, she embraces his concept of 'the Good' and this aspect of Platonic philosophy is frequently reflected in her novels.
Her most recent philosophical work, *Metaphysics as a Guide to
Morals* (1992), in a much wider-ranging discussion, addresses some
of the problems which have absorbed so much of her interest in
the novels, particularly those from *The Time of the Angels* onwards,
that is, how we can approach the idea of morality in human life
now that its religious foundations have been largely snatched from
us; it is, again, based on Platonic theories which serve to underpin
Murdoch's ideas and to refute the scepticism of modern 'structuralist'
philosophers.

The problem of religion has loomed large in Murdoch's philosophical thought and is a significant influence in her novels. She
was brought up as a Protestant; as a child she was taught to pray
and the doctrine of the Trinity was explained to her at an early age.
From her early belief, she moved through Marxism to an agnostic
standpoint, believing in nothing supernatural, rejecting God, not
accepting the divinity of Christ and having no faith in the idea of a
personal God; religion for her is to do with spiritual change and
renewal of life and it is this view which has become increasingly

significant in the later novels, connecting up with her acceptance of Plato's idea of Man's life being a pilgrimage towards reality. She is very aware, however, of the comfort of religion: 'To present the idea of God at all', she explains, 'even as myth, is a consolation' and she sees art as able to develop imaginative structures to compensate Man for the absence of God (*FAS*, p. 88). Today she sees herself as a Christian 'fellow-traveller', accepting the reality of the *persona* of Christ as a kind of moral exemplum, though not as a supernatural being.

Murdoch has tried her hand at many different forms of writing. Apart from the novels and philosophical books, she has published plays, poems, a short story, the libretto of an opera, *The Servants*, for which composer William Mathias wrote the music, and a 'play with music', *The One Alone*, which was performed on BBC Radio 3 in 1987. Her first two plays, each written in conjunction with another writer, were based on her own novels, *A Severed Head* (1964) and *The Italian Girl* (1968). The two later plays, *The Servants and the Snow*, which was the original for *The Servants*, and *The Three Arrows* were first performed respectively in 1970 and 1972 and published together in book form in 1973; she has also made a dramatic adaptation of *The Black Prince*.

Like many famous people she has written her fair share of letters to *The Times*; a number of these have been concerned with education, particularly with the education of girls and the question of selective versus comprehensive schools, in which latter argument she comes down heavily on the side of selection. Education does not, in fact, play a major part in her novels but *The Sandcastle* is set in a boys' school and the question of girls' education and also of choice occurs in that novel as well as in several others (see, for instance, *The Flight from the Enchanter*, and *The Green Knight*).

Unquestionably, Murdoch's fame and skill rest in her novels but she herself claimed in the discussions in Caen that she 'would much rather be a poet', apparently seeing novel-writing as a less happy destiny than that of being a poet (*Rencontres*, pp. 90f.). Earlier, in *A Word Child*, in a conversation between Hilary and Arthur, there is a brief discussion of the relative merits of plays, novels and poetry and Arthur, the 'good' character, remarks 'Poetry is best of all. Who wouldn't rather be a poet than anything else? Poetry is where words end' (p. 88).

Murdoch has some poetic gift and in the past fifteen years has published a number of poems in magazines, as well as a little volume entitled *A Year of Birds* (1978) which, with its delicate wood engravings by her friend Reynolds Stone,[6] can be seen as a delightfully pleasing 'coffee-table' edition but perhaps little more. Certainly if we expect poetry that reflects the mind behind the novels we shall be disappointed, though the acutely sensitive observation of birds throughout the months of the year chimes in well with the eye for detail displayed in the novels. There is an obvious interest in a variety of poetic possibilities and a technical competence which avoids the obtrusion of rhyme or of rhythmic patterns and ensures that the poems are in tune with the fragile delicacy of the engravings:

> When the dark hawberries hang down and drip like blood
> And the old man's beard has climbed up high in the wood
> And the golden bracken has been broken by the snows
> And Jesus Christ has come again to heal and pardon,
> Then the little robin follows me through the garden,
> In the dark days his breast is like a rose. ('December')

The touch is light but there is a lack of substance in the book, reflected perhaps in the lines quoted above; the sombre tone of the first three lines, the almost ominous vocabulary – 'dark . . . drip like blood . . . broken' leads only to the homely picture of the garden robin which brightens up the dark days of December. Indeed, perhaps we should not expect it to lead elsewhere; the poems and the illustrations that go with them were, as the dustjacket of the 1984 edition makes clear, 'originally conceived as a calendar'. It is an interesting little publication, however, and the poems have been set to music by composer Malcolm Williamson. Murdoch also had some leanings towards being a painter and in her 1983 interview with John Haffenden (p. 199) remarked 'I envy painters, I think they are happy people'.

The two original plays are more substantial than the poetry and deal with themes familiar to us through the novels – the nature of love and of truth and the problems of power. The first, *The Servants and the Snow*, is set in some indeterminate legendary past and the geographical background is just as vague. The names of the characters appear to represent many nationalities: Basil, Oriane, Marina,

Grundig, Peter Jack, Patrice, and so on. The intention is perhaps to universalise the fable and to make it applicable to all who are involved in domination of a feudal kind; it is disturbing, though sadly familiar still in the twentieth-century world, that after the death of the 'new liberal' Basil, a fresh tyranny appears to be about to open up under General Klein. The enigmatic mime at the end, with Frederic closing the romance he has been reading and shutting himself in the cupboard as the stage darkens, underlines the idea of the play as *fabula* and is itself a curious reversal of a frequent device in the novels; there we shall see how the story is again and again presented to us as something that is being performed, whereas here the performance ends with the implication that it is all just a story that Frederic has been reading.

The play is about love and revenge, about mercy – or the lack of mercy – about responsibility and about the power of the past and of tradition. Mikey's death near the end of the play brings about a train of consequences which result in two further deaths – those of Peter Jack and of Basil – but Maxim's words to Basil contain the central philosophical message concerning the concept of subjugation and domination:

> while there are masters and servants joint responsibility means nothing. I accuse you. You are pleased to be our figure-head and our sovereign. Keep your sovereignty then and keep its consequences as well. You can die for us all (p. 109).

Nevertheless, Maxim has not reckoned with love and loyalty, for Peter Jack dies first, for Basil; nor have hatred and jealousy come into his reckoning, for Basil dies, not for them all, but at the hands of his wife who purports to believe herself betrayed. The ending of the play is a marvellous illustration of Murdoch's belief in contingency, for the fortuitous death of Mikey brings into sharp focus all the pent-up resentments of the servants for their masters; reason and justice cease to have any power and chaos is come again.

The violence with which *The Servants and the Snow* ends reminds us of the violence in the novels written about this time and it spills over into the later play, *The Three Arrows*, which is set in medieval Japan. This play is an investigation into political power and examines the precarious balance achieved between warring factions which wish to become supreme; it also highlights the problems of loyalty and treachery in a state governed by the uncontrolled emotions of individual power politics. Romance, though it plays a slight part in the fortunes of the characters, is no more than a digression from the main plot. The Princess Keiko dies for love, or for lost love, but her would-be lover, Yorimitsu, having rejected 'the paths of action and of holiness', has not truly 'chosen the path of love'; offered personal freedom or marriage to the princess but continued captivity, he finally chooses what he sees as his chance for freedom and escapes from imprisonment at the expense of Keiko's life. ('Freedom is a mixed concept', Murdoch comments in *The Sovereignty of Good* (pp. 100–1).) The dilemma posited here reappears in various forms in the novels, for it is the dilemma that Murdoch sees as bedevilling all forms of modern art – that between 'sincerity' and 'truth' and between 'freedom' and 'love'. The novels, however, are peculiarly free of direct political motivation, the plays being the only overt expression of such a theme in Murdoch's work.

These two plays are very deliberately set in a time and a place which feed myth. They are essentially artificial, 'staged' as spectacles, distanced from the lives of the audience. They have a peculiarly unmodern feel about them. Plays of this kind would not alone have brought popularity and fame to their author, though they are of interest in supporting and emphasising some of the themes of her novels. On the other hand, the novels deal with contemporary life and are nothing if not dramatic, yet when they are turned into plays, even dramatisations which Murdoch herself has overseen, they are a little disappointing, lacking both the depth and the breadth of their originals.

As a novelist Murdoch has been prolific and, despite her comments in 1978 about the superiority of poetry (see p. 11 above), by 1988, in the British Council pamphlet about her, she wrote of the novel, 'This supreme literary form is . . . only now beginning its reign; long may it travel with us.' It appears as a declaration of personal faith in the novel form, in defiance of those who have claimed that the novel is dead. By that time she herself had written twenty-three novels but, equally importantly, she has always been an avid reader of novels and other literature, both European and classical; she reads and re-reads her favourite Victorians – Jane Austen, Dickens, George Eliot and particularly Henry James whose interest in 'patterns' has influenced her own novels. On the other hand, she claims not to read the novels of most of her contemporaries, despite her vibrant support for the strength of the novel form today.

It is perhaps always invidious to attempt to classify a novelist's work into chronological periods; such a classification however, has the virtue of simplicity and can help to suggest change and growth as it is seen in the novels over the whole of the novelist's career. The thematic approach, particularly in a novelist of Murdoch's vast output, is an attractive alternative but I have decided in this book to use the simpler method in order to be able to contain what I have to say within the permitted bounds.

The first period I shall deal with is that of the 1950s in which the four novels from *Under the Net* (1954) to *The Bell* (1958) are examined; secondly, the brief romantic period of the early 1960s, from *A Severed Head* (1961) to *The Red and the Green* (1965) will be looked at as a time of transition leading to the more substantial central period of the late 1960s and early 1970s, from *The Time of the Angels* (1966) to *An Accidental Man* (1971); in these novels moral and spiritual violence are of increasing significance and the concept of evil is realised; the novels from *The Black Prince* (1973) to *Henry and Cato* (1976), though still violent, bring the protagonists to understand more clearly the limits of freedom and to recognise the meaning of love. In particular, these novels show a more deliberate interest in the problems of narration and narrative devices. The next period, that of the late 1970s and 1980s begins with *The Sea, The Sea* (1978) and considers the six novels up to *The Message to the Planet* (1989); in these novels the influence of Platonic philosophy is increasingly apparent, with an emphasis on the movement away from ordinary human love towards a more universal spiritual love; the frame of reference for the novels is akin to religion as the characters look outside themselves for solutions to their problems. The survey is brought up to date with a chapter on *The Green Knight* (1993), in which myth and reality are so closely intertwined that the readers find themselves sucked into a world in which mystic events seem to be inseparable from those of the natural world.

Are there ways in which Murdoch's other interests impinge upon the matter discussed in her novels? Despite her admiration for poetry, she is not in general a poetic novelist, though some of her later

novels have moved towards the poetic in their descriptive passages.
We can observe, however, that when one of her characters is a writer
– and this is frequently the case – he or she is usually a novelist,
not a poet or a dramatist, though in *Bruno's Dream* Miles, who has
struggled with poetry during his early life, ends up as a poet, as
does Julian in *The Black Prince*, whilst Lucius Lamb in *Henry and
Cato* is, or has been, an unsuccessful poet and James in *The Sea,
The Sea* turns out to have been a secret poet when, after his death,
Charles discovers his poems 'neatly typed out' and, like Murdoch's
novels, 'filling several large looseleaf books' (*The Sea*, p. 483).

There are, however, many dramatic moments in the novels and
the fact that several of them have already been turned into plays
and television films suggests the author's interest in drama. In our
discussion of the novels it will be seen, too, that the plots are often
presented in terms of drama with the reader looking in upon them
as on a play, knowing that there is a life outside the action for
everyone concerned but momentarily suspending disbelief. The influence of drama is further apparent in the close parallels that are
made with Shakespeare's plays in a number of the novels. Murdoch
herself commented in her interview with John Haffenden, 'of course
a novel is a drama' (Haffenden, p. 204), and later in a discussion
with John Bayley and Martin Dodsworth at the British Academy in
1991 she remarked that there is 'great religious power in Shakespeare'; it thus seems meaningful to look at the way in which her
novels tend towards the dramatic.

In any discussion of the novels, however, the major question is
whether Murdoch is, as some critics have described her, a philosophical novelist. If this means are her books about ideas, then she
undoubtedly is, but this is to look at the problem too simplistically.
The dichotomy she herself posits between *being* a philosopher and
teaching philosophy (see p. 8 above) seems to be equally relevant
to this question. She herself appears to consider the purely philosophical novel as an unsatisfactory art form and in the first chapter of *Sartre, Romantic Rationalist* she suggests the shortcomings
of the 'philosophical' novel by comparing Sartre's *La Nausée*, to
its disadvantage, with Kafka's *The Castle*:

> *La Nausée* is not a metaphysical tale, like *The Castle*, nor is the
> absurdity of Sartre the absurdity of Kafka. Kafka's K. is not himself

a metaphysician; his actions show forth, but his thoughts do not analyse, the absurdity of his world. The hero of *La Nausée* is reflective and analytical; the book is not a metaphysical image so much as a philosophical analysis which makes use of the metaphysical image. . . .

She concludes this part of the discussion with the comment, 'Roquentin's [*La Nausée*] plight appears to be a philosopher's plight, while K's [*The Castle*] is that of everyman' (*SRR*, pp. 48–9). It is everyman's plight which she attempts to grapple with in her own novels. Any analysis which her characters make of the absurdity of their own world is subordinate to their actions, and though the characters' dilemmas constantly bring ideas into the forefront of the novels it is their interaction with other characters and with the world around them that is of ultimate significance. In her final summing-up she remarks, 'The novel, the novel proper that is, is about people's treatment of each other, and so it is about human values' (*SRR*, p. 138) and she ends by commenting:

[Sartre's] inability to write a great novel is a tragic symptom of a situation which afflicts us all. We know that the real lesson to be taught is that the human person is precious and unique; but we seem unable to set it forth except in terms of ideology and abstraction (*SRR*, p. 148).

At the time of writing *Sartre, Romantic Rationalist* Murdoch had had no novel accepted for publication. Her words, however, suggest what she would wish to put forward in her novels and this was not the concept of the isolated Sartrean man but the idea of the interdependence of people in a contingent world. Particularly in the first-person novels she does present the isolated world of the self-absorbed solipsistic man but only to show us that finally his plight is the plight of everyman. The chapters which follow will show to what extent Murdoch's attitudes have changed or remained the same over the forty years since she published her first novel.

Whatever else may have changed, her actual method of writing her novels is the same as it has always been. It is perhaps particularly important in such complicated plots that all the details are carefully planned in advance. Such planning – characters, settings, incidents, the general shape of the novel – is completed before Murdoch begins to write. When she has the overall plan clear in her mind she is able to begin writing it, by hand, on lined paper, either in notebooks or on loose-leaf sheets. She revises the first draft extensively and follows it with a final draft, also hand-written. Despite the widespread use of word-processors, she does not use one and has no intention of doing so. She says that she enjoys writing and cannot quite imagine life without having a novel 'on the go'.

2

The Early Novels

In a Book Trust pamphlet published about her in 1988,[1] Iris Murdoch wrote:

> Novels are individuals, about individuals, essentially comic, essentially sad, telling of the secret travail which ordinary life conceals, and formulating deep truths about human society and the human soul. They are also works of art.

Since the publication of her first novel, *Under the Net*, in 1954, she has constantly illustrated the enormous breadth of possibilities within the novel. The individual novels and the individuals within the novels display between them the whole gamut of human experience and human emotions; comedy and tragedy exist side by side and the extremes of behaviour and the intricacies of relationships serve only to highlight the actualities of ordinary life in which we strive towards fuller understanding of ourselves and consequently of the world around us. The novels are metaphors of life and consciously presented as art, so that the reality of life is subsumed into the theatricality of an invented world.

Like the playwright, Murdoch prepares the stage and sets the scene for her dramas, creating a world of 'them' and 'us', enabling us, as audience, to look in upon the lives of her characters, simultaneously knowing that we are being told a story and yet consciously suspending our disbelief and feeling the essential reality of the events that pass before us. The four novels of the 1950s, *Under the Net*

(1954), *The Flight from the Enchanter* (1956), *The Sandcastle* (1957)
and *The Bell* (1958) all share a slightly claustrophobic atmosphere
in which their characters are isolated as on a stage so that our attention is not deflected by the irrelevancies of life surrounding them.
The Sandcastle and *the Bell*, like several of the later novels,[2] are
set in enclosed communities, but even in the first two novels, which
appear to be set solidly in the vast metropolis of London there is
often a similar sense of confinement. When, in the opening chapter
of *Under the Net*, Jake meets Finn in Earls Court Road after what
must have been a crowded boat journey from Dieppe to Newhaven
and an equally crowded train journey up to London, it is as though
they are alone, shut into their lives together. In Jake's mind is a
picture of Finn leaning against a doorpost with his eyes closed, shutting
out the world, and Jake himself talks of burying his 'head so deep
in dear London that I can forget that I have ever been away' (*UTN*,
p. 7). Bustling Earls Court Road is reduced to an island where two
men sit alone on cases in the middle of the pavement, oblivious of
all around them, whilst they try to readjust their world which seems
to have fallen about their ears.

The *Flight from the Enchanter* opens with Annette Cockeyne's
decision to leave her 'expensive finishing-school in Kensington'
(p. 7); when she walks out of her Italian class there is no sense of
the presence of other students but only of Annette herself as she
fulfils her bizarre desire to swing on the chandelier in the dining-
room and as she gravely presents to the Headmistress the leather-
bound volume of Browning which she has just stolen from the school
library. The plot moves easily from the enclosed surroundings of
Annette's school to what one would expect to be the more open life
of Kensington but the shift is really toward equally enclosed so-
cieties – the miniature publishing project of the *Artemis* and Rosa's
suffocating relationship with the Lusiewicz brothers.

The symbolic titles of both novels reinforce the sense of restric-
tion, of being hemmed in, of the desire for freedom, and they underline the basic theme of imprisonment and escape which is common
to most of Murdoch's novels: 'freedom is only an idea', comments
Jake to Dave Gellman (*UTN*, p. 27); in Murdoch's novels it is also,
too often, an illusion; physical confinement is not a necessary ad-
junct of enslavement; moral and spiritual compulsions are more
devastating and the 'spellbinders' of the novels ensnare the hearts

and minds of those around them as surely as the settings enclose them. The phrase 'under the net' is used by Hugo in the novel (or by Hugo in the guise of Annandine) as a position to which the truth-seeker aspires:

> the movement away from theory and generality is the movement towards truth. All theorizing is flight. We must be ruled by the situation itself and this is unutterably particular. Indeed it is something to which we can never get close enough, however hard we may try as it were to crawl under the net (*UTN*, pp. 80f).

The discussion which Jake reads from his philosophical book, *The Silencer*, is concerned with the nature of truth and, for Hugo, escape and flight are a retreat from truth; only by avoiding generalities and looking at the particular does he believe it possible 'to crawl under the net' and make an approach to truth. We may thus interpret the restrictive settings of Murdoch's novels as settings which are designed to facilitate the search for truth, though it is Hugo, not Murdoch, who posits this idea.

Years later, in the discussion at the University of Caen in 1978 Murdoch explained, 'The "net", of course, under which one cannot get, is the net of language' (*Rencontres*, p. 76). She went on to comment on 'language moving towards silence, and the difficulty of relating concepts to anything which lies behind them, or under them'. This is precisely the thought that Hugo expounds to Jake: 'truth can be attained . . . only in silence. It is in silence that the human spirit touches the divine' (*UTN*, p. 81). Later, he does not even recognise himself in Annandine and the ideas that Jake has taken from him appear to him 'terribly hard' to understand, though they were once his own.

Language, communication, can all too easily be used to conceal rather than to expose. Both speaker and listener place their own interpretations on what is said, understanding what they want to believe, creating through their use of words a wall of misunderstanding. Through the specific and particular we may approach closer to objective truth, though what we uncover may well be a situation that we prefer not to face. Until almost the end of the novel the characters in *Under the Net* are trapped by the net of language which has buoyed their false understanding; it is only at the end that Jake and Hugo are able to crawl from under the net, escape the trap of language and move into the silence of understanding. Yet even Hugo, with all his philosophy, would perhaps have been happier without the final knowledge vouchsafed him by the silent response of Sadie to his approaches.

Throughout the novel there are what we might see as symbolic scenes of enclosing and imprisonment: Jake and Hugo in the Cold Cure Centre; Jake in the mime theatre alone at night; Jake locked in Sadie's flat; Mister Mars in the cage in Sammy's flat; Hugo suffering from concussion in the hospital. The setting of the mime-theatre scene is itself a reminder that art and life are inextricably intertwined; Jake's search for Anna has led him to the little 'Riverside Miming Theatre' where she has created for herself a theory of 'pure art', based on second-hand ideas she has absorbed from Hugo. Her very involvement in the theatre is a retreat from truth (Hugo later describes it as 'a sort of a lie' (*UTN*, p. 222)), for Anna accepts it as a loving tribute from Hugo, though she knows that he has no love to spare for her, only for her sister Sadie. Furthermore, she has sacrificed her own art for the sake of involving herself in an art which, she believes, reflects Hugo's interests. Physical confinement, however, often serves to enlarge the mind and the imagination; for Jake, the concept of truth is first posited in the Cold Cure Centre and finally discovered in the enclosed confines of Hugo's room in the hospital, where also he is brought to understand the reasons for his own imprisonment in Sadie's flat.

The artifice involved in imprisonment, rescue and escape brings the incidents directly into the contrived realms of story or theatre. We become audience, rather than participator, in the bizarre theft of Mister Mars, in Finn's skilful use of a hairpin to release Jake from Sadie's flat and in the melodramatic events leading up to Hugo's flight from the hospital. Yet we live through the events, too, as we live through the blinding of Gloucester or the death of Desdemona in the theatre.

The interest in dramatic art is reinforced by Anna's life; when Jake first met her, she and Sadie 'did a singing act' (*UTN*, p. 29) but at the Riverside Theatre she has allowed her newly-acquired theories to destroy her old life and to persuade her that the old form of her art – her singing – lacked truth, was 'corrupt'; as she explains this to Jake he senses 'the curious artificiality in her tone' (*UTN*, p. 41) but does not at first recognise Hugo's influence in the ideas she propounds.

The very telling of the story in the novel is itself artifice, for Jake is a writer, though not a very successful one, and one who makes his living mainly out of the second-hand art of translation, rather in the way that Anna has built her art and life on Hugo's theories. The first-person narration in the novel, however, does not rely on modern theories about what an author can do with a story which is progressing in the mind of a writer; it is straightforward narration; only the plot is complicated and convoluted. Murdoch herself has commented on the role of the first-person narrator in *A Word Child* that she did not actually make 'Hilary's telling of the story itself into part of the story' (*Rencontres*, p. 73) but rather followed an older convention; her comments appear at first apposite to the position of Jake in this novel; for most of the novel he is simply the story-teller, presenting the tale as he sees it to the reader. Yet a story-teller needs words, needs to communicate and in this novel there is a strong suggestion that words cannot communicate; though Jake tells us (see *UTN*, p. 53) that his acquaintance with Hugo is the central theme of the book, he nevertheless demonstrates the inadequacy of language by failing to make us understand his relationship with Hugo as anything more than a role he has taken on under Hugo's influence; he has misunderstood Hugo from beginning to end; he misjudges Hugo's reaction to publication of *The Silencer*; he misjudges Hugo's capacity for love and mistakes the object of his love. Moreover, only by accepting Hugo's account of events is Jake able to make any sense of his own life: 'I knew everything,' he remarks, 'I got it all the wrong way round, that's all!' (*UTN*, p. 227). To some extent then, we may see Jake's narration as 'part of the story'; his solipsistic view of life presents what he himself believes to be true; if we are to believe Hugo's account, however, the novel is deconstructed and we realise that whatever the signs may have been they did not support Jake's beliefs.

Here, from the very first novel, Murdoch involves us in questioning the nature of truth, and language itself is seen to be artifice; it can be used to display or conceal; it is itself theatre: it puts on a show which may or may not represent the speaker's true thoughts; it is interpreted by the listeners in varying ways according to their own needs. Iris Murdoch repeatedly concerns herself in her novels with art and artifice and it is this aspect of them, perhaps, that denies the appellation 'Angry Young Woman' that was foisted upon her in the 1950s. The picaresque character of Jake's adventures and the apparent rootlessness of his own character encouraged the critics to see him as a kind of 'Lucky Jim' (his adventures could never, surely, have been equated with those of John Osborne's Jimmy Porter in *Look Back in Anger*, the original 'angry young man'). Murdoch has always denied the association and the further we travel from the 1950s, the clearer it is that, whilst the novels of the 'Angry Young Men' of that time were the forerunners of the disillusioned 'University novels' of today, Murdoch was in process of creating a novelistic world unique to her own art, a world which attempts to grapple, not with the so-called social realism of the 1950s and 1960s, but rather with the malaise that lies at the heart of life, the 'real' realism in which we, all of us, have faced the changes in society forced upon us by the Second World War, by the holocaust, by the fear of the atom bomb, by the gradual erosion (however much it may be denied) of the old class system wherein one's role in life was essentially dictated by one's parents' income and social standing. Of course, as time goes by and novel follows novel, Murdoch moves on from this position but it is a kind of starting-point that separates her from the other novelists of the 1950s.

The second novel, *The Flight from the Enchanter,* has what we may think of theatrically as a full supporting cast. The plot is extremely intricate, built not on the picaresque adventures of one character as in *Under the Net* but rather on the complicated interrelationships of a group. At the centre is Mischa Fox, the 'enchanter', who appears to be the puppet-master, pulling the strings, though neither we nor the other characters are fully aware of this until almost the end when Mischa and his *alter ego*, Calvin Blick, destroy Rosa's illusions. Again the claustrophobic scenes are set before us – for example, Hunter's *Artemis* office, Peter Saward's study, the Lusiewicz brothers' bed-sitting room – and again, language fails to illuminate thoughts: 'One reads the signs as best one can,' remarks Peter Saward on the last page of the book, 'and one may be totally misled'. For Peter himself, for the Lusiewicz brothers, for John Rainborough, for Rosa, for Annette, for Nina the signs have indeed misled.

This novel is, perhaps, the most difficult and the most puzzling of the early novels because, though dealing with significant social, political and philosophical concepts, it often appears to be rather remote from real life. The characters are a gathering of outcasts from society, none of whom seems to be fully realized: the refugees – Mischa Fox himself, Nina, Jan and Stefan, the tubercular Peter Saward; the rootless misfit Annette; the outworn old ladies from the Suffragette Movement; even Rosa, enchanted by Mischa, ominously enthralled by the Lusiewicz brothers, lacks solidity. Over twenty years later in the Gifford lectures (1982) Murdoch stated unequivocally, 'In good art we do not ask for realism; we ask for truth.' The truth of *The Flight from the Enchanter* lies in its solutions to the problems which the characters have faced and its realism in our awareness of the emotional dimension.

A new moral order is restored to Rosa's life by the removal from the scene of the illegal immigrants Jan and Stefan, but the same political guile destroys Nina who becomes the innocent victim, the scapegoat who suffers not merely for the sins of others but also for their neglect; Rosa finally returns from Italy, free of the moral and emotional ties which have bound her to Mischa; Peter Saward is able to reject her offer of marriage because he knows that Rosa is merely seeking a safety-net, but his attempt to comfort her as the novel ends establishes the truth and perhaps also, at last, the reality of Mischa's life: '"See," he said, "here is the old market-square and here is the famous bronze fountain, and here is the medieval bridge across the river. . . . And here is the cathedral . . ."' (*FE*, p. 287). Until now Mischa has been a mystery figure; early in the novel Rainborough outlined the lack of information about him:

No one knows his age. No one knows where he came from either. Where was he born? What blood is in his veins? No one knows. And if you try to imagine you are paralysed. It's like that thing with his eyes. You can't look into his eyes. You have to look *at* his eyes. Heaven knows what you'd see if you looked in (*FE*, p. 35).

As Peter displays the photographs, Mischa becomes 'de-mystified' by the imposition of his childhood background, a background which has the reality and solidity of the past and which gives him a place in the world that Rosa is able to understand; it is a fitting irony, too, that whilst the compromising photographs of Rosa with the Lusiewicz brothers served to separate her from Mischa, the photographs from his childhood serve to help her to know him better. The photographs, like the frequent dramatic scenes in the novels, act as a parallel to real life; they are life deprived of its emotional dimension; thus, through them, Rosa is compelled first to reassess her relationship with the Lusiewicz brothers and next to see Mischa in a simple and human context.

Perhaps serving as an antidote to the mystifications and complications of *The Flight from the Enchanter*, *The Sandcastle* is the most conventional of the early novels. It is set almost entirely in the enclosed community of St Bride's, a boys' boarding school in the country south of London; its principal actors are the staff and boys of the school and Rain Carter, a young painter who, as an outsider, intrudes upon and interrupts the steady routine of St Bride's. Whilst the relationships are not unusual – for it is nothing for a middle-aged man to believe himself in love with a vulnerable woman half his age or for that woman, having recently lost a father to whom she was devoted, to believe in her turn that she too is in love – they nevertheless exist in an atmosphere of fantasy. This is emphasized by the slightly fey figure of Felicity with her belief in magic, by the mysterious appearances of the gypsy and by the symbolic title of the novel – the sandcastle which Mor and Rain build is inevitably destroyed at the turn of the tide.

The theatricality of the novel maintains a sort of continuity with what has gone before. Incidents such as the slow descent of Rain Carter's car into the river or the rescue of Donald from the tower are described with the same minute, absorbing and ingenious detail that accompanied the abduction of Mr Mars from Sammy's flat in *Under the Net*. At the end, however, normality is restored more solidly and more traditionally than in either of the two previous novels; Rain, the outsider, has disappeared from the scene, the Mor family are back together again, Donald is to be allowed to work with Tim Burke, Felicity is being given the chance of a university education and Mor himself is well on his way to becoming a Member of Parliament. All the loose ends are tied up and 'Everything was all right now' (*TS*, p. 313). Even Felicity's tears seem to be tears of relief that her worries over her parents and her brother are at last resolved. This novel, with its final reinforcement of family values, sits rather uncertainly in the midst of the more turbulent presentation of relationships that can be seen as typically Murdochian; it is too predictable and the combination of fantasy and reality are only precariously acceptable.

The best of the novels of this early period is the last of the four, *The Bell*. A third-person novel, like the two which precede it, the novel begins with a brief survey of Dora Greenfield's life up to the moment when we see her travelling in a train to rejoin her estranged husband, Paul, after a six-month separation. The events of the first chapter are seen almost entirely through Dora's eyes and it is soon evident that she is dominated by Paul to the complete subjugation of her own personality. Her attempt to leave him had been an attempt to escape the shackles of her incompatible marriage and return to what she saw as the carefree happiness she had experienced as an art student at the Slade. Her whole stream of thought suggests that Paul had acquired a wife in the same spirit as he collects medieval artefacts; Dora, like his treasures, was 'installed in [his] Knightsbridge flat, in the midst of [his] unique collection of medieval ivories' (*The Bell*, p. 8). There she felt herself imprisoned and consequently set her mind on the idea of escape from the 'elegant and untouchable flat' (*The Bell*, p. 11) until at last she took flight and left him.

Paul himself is at odds with his surroundings; he is constantly associated with the word 'violence': he is 'a violent man'; he creates violent scenes; he acts with 'violent and predatory gestures'; he sets traps for Dora and oscillates 'between brutality and sentimentality' (*The Bell*, p. 11). Dora's attempt to escape from him is unsuccessful because her personality has been so completely subdued that she no longer knows who she is and is almost incapable of making up her own mind. Furthermore, as we have seen in the earlier novels, physical escape is not freedom and Dora is still enslaved to her vision of Paul, a bond which cannot be broken by mere absence from him; neither, as soon becomes apparent, can it be broken by the misery of reassociation with him. The almost palpable tie established between husband and wife, faint in *The Sandcastle*, stronger here, is a major theme in the group of novels

which follows *The Bell*. The train journey to Pemberton and to reunion with Paul ends with a metaphor of freedom: Dora rescues a
Red Admiral butterfly, trapped in the carriage and in danger of
destruction; at the very moment of her own re-imprisonment, in a
theatrical gesture, she gives the butterfly its liberty by releasing it
into the air. We might perhaps see this as a very fragile metaphor,
and yet double-edged, for the butterfly's life is at the best transi-
tory and the restoration of its liberty is all too like Dora's own
experiences.

   For Dora, on her arrival at Pemberton, physical confinement is
added to her mental and spiritual confinement; Imber Court is surrounded by 'an enormous stone wall' (*The Bell*, p. 26) and entered
through 'tall iron gates' (*The Bell,* p. 27). Yet she herself had found
no genuine freedom in her original flight from Paul and it is in the
enclosed community of Imber court and its silence that she begins
to come to terms with her own life. Paul's hectoring attempt at
domination after the cataclysmic events surrounding the intended
inauguration of the new bell helps Dora to understand the value of
silence; when she destroys the two letters that began and ended her
affair with Paul she frees herself of all that lay between them. Her
return to the placidity of life at Imber Court with Michael and her
talks with Mother Clare help her to find herself again; she goes
back to her painting and at the end of the novel she is left alone in
the stillness and silence of Imber, though even now, we might notice, with false illusions, for she remains convinced that Michael
intends to marry Catherine. Yet her immediate future is assured;
she will neither return to Paul nor go again to Noel but will build
her own life, return to her art studies, live in Sally's flat and perhaps become a teacher.

   Our introduction to Imber Court in Chapter 2 details the house
and its setting; from Mrs Mark we learn the names of its inhabitants but through Dora's eyes we see them as people. The architec-
ture of Imber Court contends for our interest and Paul as art critic
and scholar is in one way the descendant of Jake; just as Jake strives
himself to be creator but lives parasitically on the translations he
makes of the novels of his French contemporary, Jean-Pierre Breteuil,
so Paul sponges on true art. When Jean-Pierre's novel, *Nous les
Vainqueurs*, wins the Prix-Goncourt, however, Jake faces up to his
own past and future, whereas, even at the dissolution of the com-

munity after the debâcle with the new bell, Paul's energies are absorbed, not by helping to put things right, not by reassessing his own part in the troubled relationship between himself and Dora, but by dedicating himself to the interpretation of the inscriptions on the resurrected old bell. Dora's paintings are, at least, her own, though Paul tries to stifle her individuality. It is fitting that Paul goes off to London at the end of the novel and the reader knows nothing of his future, for we do not really care about him.

The sense of theatricality is strong in this novel and the reader is joined by Dora as onlooker for she is the 'outsider', a character-type who is of considerable significance in a number of Murdoch's later novels; her predecessor is Rain Carter in *The Sandcastle* who, unknowingly, acts as the catalyst for the dramatic events in that novel. Dora comes in from a world outside Imber Court and succeeds, albeit unintentionally, in destroying the community. Her first view of the house is presented rather like a stage setting for a Shakespearean performance, as though from a darkened auditorium she waits for the play to begin:

> The avenue [i.e. where Dora was] was dark, but the house stood beyond it with the declining sun slanting across its front. It was a very pale grey, and with a colourless sky of evening light behind it, it had the washed brilliance of a print. In the centre of the facade a high pediment supported by four pillars rose over the line of the roof. A green copper dome curved above. At the first floor level the pillars ended at a balustrade, and from there a pair of stone staircases swept in two great curves to the ground (*The Bell*, pp. 27f.).

The next three or four pages are filled with views through Dora's eyes; the words 'Dora saw' constantly recur until, as she enters the house we are again overcome by the sense that she is entering a theatre:

> The tall doorway ahead of her led into a large hall. All was rather dark within, as no lights had been turned on yet. Dora . . . got an impression of a great staircase and of people hurrying through the hall and out by another door at the far end (*The Bell*, pp. 30f.).

A moment later she enters the chapel; the scene before her 'seemed . . . slightly dramatic' (*The Bell*, p. 32) and makes her catch her breath; the inevitable dramatic associations with a religious ceremony en- sue as Dora is slipped into 'the back row' and watches 'the relig- ious scene' unfold before her. When she next enters the chapel, even in the broad light of the following day, what she sees appears to her like the 'aftermath of amateur theatricals' (*The Bell*, p. 62).

The narrative method again and again gives us this double view of the plot which is so disconcerting for the reader. Though Dora is a character in the novel she is also an onlooker, like us part of the theatre audience, and her dual role contains within it the seeds both of reality and of theatricality. We have this same feeling of uncer- tainty during Michael Meade's nightmare as he watches what he believes to be the 'final scene' of some strange disaster (*The Bell*, p. 78). Yet the sense of *déjà vu* we receive when we come to the opening of Chapter 18 only partially prepares us for the grand fi- nale of the actual climax. In the wings, as it were, we wait for the action, with Dora as both playwright and actress. The stage has already been set, the play almost written. Dora is determined to 'Make a miracle . . .', though she knows that her 'miracle' is noth- ing more than a theatrical device. 'Nothing is too difficult,' she tells Toby, ' . . . With an engineer to help me, I can do anything'; but in her mind she has created a new role for herself: 'In this holy community she would play the witch' (*The Bell*, pp. 198f.). The confusion of roles between Toby and Nick, however, results in the latter acting as the sorcerer's apprentice in a dénouement which even he has only partly foreseen.

The characters in this novel are more fully realised on a human scale than most of the characters of earlier novels; at the same time they have a symbolic function. The first of the series of twins to appear in Murdoch's novels, it could be assumed that Catherine and Nick Fawley represent respectively Good and Evil; Catherine, beauti- ful, quiet, 'our little saint', a postulant to enter through the gates of Imber Abbey, appears to be in marked contrast to Nick, dark, slightly satanic-looking, a drunkard whose homosexual past has turned sour upon him. Yet both are tainted by love and ironically for the same man, Michael Meade; yet it is not really love that taints, as they both appear to believe, but the failure to acknowledge it, and for this failure atonement is necessary before redemption can be achieved. Nick's sin, however, is more potent than Catherine's for not only does he fail to acknowledge love but he has betrayed it and his betrayal haunts him to the death.

The only people in Imber Court who know the story of the fourteenth-century bell of Imber are Paul, Dora and Catherine. The recounting of the legend of the guilty nun and her death in the lake which followed the symbolic drowning of the bell is intended by Paul as a moral lesson to Dora; but Dora has been quite frank about her affair with Noel Spens; the significance of the legend is much more apposite to the situation of Catherine, about to become a bride of Christ, yet tainted by her unconfessed human love for Michael. When for the second time in seven hundred years the abbey bell falls into the lake, Catherine feels that it is a judgement upon her and tries to drown herself like the guilty nun before her. It is the arch-contriver Nick, however, who has twice betrayed Michael, who successfully kills himself – the perfect revenge, as Michael sees it, for lost love. At the same time, however, we may see it as the final retribution: in engineering the destruction of Michael's dream, Nick drives Catherine mad and consequently himself embraces death, unredeemed by love.

The theme of love is especially significant in *The Bell* for it transcends the physical and the human and moves into the realm of the religious and the spiritual. Much of the spiritual weight of the novel falls upon Michael Meade for not only are both Fawleys corrupted by their love for him but he himself has been unable to reconcile human with spiritual love. His life as leader of the community at Imber Court is for him a retreat from reality; it fulfils for him neither his vocation of teacher, nor his desire to be a priest; at the same time, though he has suppressed his past, he has not escaped it. Only by reliving his guilt with Nick, first through Toby and afterwards through Catherine, is he able to see his way to following the path of reconciliation, expressed in the words of Julian of Norwich, when 'All would yet be well' (*The Bell*, p. 291). It is too late, however, for him to make his peace with Nick and to offer him real human love:

> Nick had needed love, and he ought to have given him what he had to offer, without fears about its imperfection. If he had had more faith he would have done so, not calculating either Nick's

faults or his own. . . . So great a love must have contained some grain of good, something at least which might have attached Nick to this world, given him some glimpse of hope (*The Bell*, p. 307).

Whether Michael himself achieves redemption is unsure; 'there is a God, but I do not believe in Him', he concludes after the catastrophe (*The Bell*, p. 308) but he does go back into the real world, if it is only as a temporary teacher.

The Bell may be seen as a perfect fusion of the real and the symbolic. The skilfully patterned symbolic framework is used to reflect on the lives of the characters. A. S. Byatt comments on 'the solid life' of this novel and compares it favourably with *The Flight from the Enchanter*:

> The characters are not tied up neatly at the end of the book; they have a life of their own which exists beyond it. What will happen to Michael Meade, or to Dora, is a matter for real concern and speculation, as what will happen to Rosa is not. . . .[3]

The neat tying-up of characters at the end of a novel is often a problem for Murdoch – not that she cannot do it but that she does it too glibly. Apart from *The Sandcastle*, however, it seems to me that the early novels are less inclined to this fault than the group of romantic novels which follows. Particular problems may have been solved for Jake or for Rosa but their future life remains an enigma for the reader, though Hugo's future is settled and the other enchanter, Mischa, like Prospero loses his power to enchant.

In these four early novels, though her narrative methods have differed and though the technique has progressed, Murdoch has begun her lifelong search for truth. For her, the novel is concerned not with introspection and *angoisse* but with interrelationships, person with person. It is partly for this reason that her novels have a tendency towards the dramatic; drama is essentially about characters interacting with each other and, in order perhaps to combat the Sartrean view of isolated man, she constantly describes scenes in which the characters are of necessity responding to each other's actions. In her essay 'Against Dryness', she concludes:

We need to return from the self-centred concept of sincerity to the other-centred concept of truth. We are not isolated free choosers, monarchs of all we survey, but benighted creatures sunk in a reality whose nature we are constantly and overwhelmingly tempted to deform by fantasy (Bradbury, p. 29).

This statement may be seen not merely as a positive affirmation of her intentions in her novels, but also as a refutation of existentialist theories. We should notice, too, the use of the phrase, 'deform by fantasy' because in these early novels Murdoch may be seen moving away from fantasy towards a much more solid use of imagination.

In *Under the Net* we can see how Jake is brought from the position of deforming reality by fantasy to an understanding of the 'other-centred concept of truth'. At first, as we watch his attempts to interpret the world through his own hopes and beliefs, we might perhaps view him as a Sartrean man who understands the lives of others only as they are reflected in his own life, who in effect, suffers the anguish of his own indecision: he has lived in Madge's flat but has not looked after her; Finn he sees as 'an inhabitant of my universe, and [I] cannot conceive that he has one containing me' (*UTN*, p. 9); when Madge throws him out he cannot decide where to go. We soon realise, however, that he is not existential man but selfish and solipsistic man; he entirely invents the roles of others around him, basing them on his own beliefs. Thus he continues to live in a fantasy world of his own invention until the moment when he is faced with the truth in Hugo's room in the hospital. It is the end of the drama and though Jake is reluctant to relinquish it, he has to acknowledge that life moves on:

I wanted to hold on, just a little longer, to my last act. A premonition of pain made me delay; the pain that comes after the drama, when the bodies have been carried from the stage and the trumpets are silent and an empty day dawns which will dawn again and again to mock our contrived finalities (*UTN*, p. 239).

It is a declaration against life having the 'sufficient reason' he had opted for in Chapter 2, an affirmation of the contingency which he had then rejected.

Under the Net has, perhaps, a more direct affinity with Murdoch's philosophical thought in the 1950s than the novels which follow. Not only does it seem to be designed to negate the truth of Sartre's perception of character in his novels but it is also in itself a novel which, for all its lightheartedness is deeply involved with philosophic ideas; both Hugo and Dave Gellman are philosophers of a kind, Dave professionally and Hugo through personal dedication to thought. The latter's ideas about language owe much to the later theories of Wittgenstein, whose posthumous *Philosophical Investigations,* published in 1953 whilst *Under the Net* was in gestation, expounded the theory that language could be meaningful only if it confined itself to the particular and to language carefully chosen to suit the subject under discussion. There is an obvious affinity with Hugo's words which Jake quotes close to the end of the novel, 'Actions don't lie, words always do' (*UTN*, p. 228). The novel is dedicated to Raymond Queneau whom Murdoch met about the same time as she met Sartre and who, she claims, was a greater influence upon her than Sartre. In discussions at Caen she remarked that this novel was influenced by Beckett and Queneau though she does not think it resembles anything by either of them (*Rencontres*, p. 76); Queneau's interest in the art of story-telling, however, may be, if only ever so slightly, reflected in the duality of the plot – Jake's original understanding and the understanding he gains through Hugo's explanations.

Inevitably any first novel will be looked at as the precursor of all that is to follow and certainly *Under the Net* has in it the seeds of many other aspects of the later novels. In particular, the interest in the concepts of truth and of love have their initial airing in this book and Murdoch's consistent emphasis on the significance of the past is seen in Jake's failure to understand his own past and its relationships; the physical and metaphorical use of the ideas of freedom and captivity are dominant, just as are the dramatic, often melodramatic, escapes associated with them.

There is a precursor of the violence which marks the novels of the 1960s in the gratuitous twisting of Anna's arm which Jake perpetrates whilst in the Mime Theatre (*UTN*, p. 41) and in the blow across the mouth which Madge inflicts on Jake when he rejects her offer of the script-writing sinecure (see *UTN*, p. 178). The cyclical pattern, later perfected in *A Word Child*, is subtly introduced through Jake's visit to Mr Tinckham in the first and the final chapters. The bizarre events and complicated relationships, the concentration on descriptive detail, the absorbing interest in the mechanics and devices of drama are also present – here the theft and release of Mr Mars and in later novels, for example, the rescue of Donald from the School Tower in *The Sandcastle*, the dredging up of the bell from the lake in *The Bell*, George's attempt to kill Rozanov in *The Philosopher's Pupil* or the journey of Anax through London in the *Green Knight*. In Hugo we have the first of the 'enchanters' who appear in the novels, though he is a pale shadow as compared with (say) Mischa Fox in the second novel, David Crimond in *The Book and the Brotherhood* or Marcus Vallar in *The Message to the Planet*. We are introduced, too, to Mr Mars, the first of many dog characters that are a feature of the novels, and which include the band of dogs in *The Sacred and Profane Love Machine* who savage Blaise Gavender, a retributive act that serves as the only apparent punishment for his sin against Harriet.

On the other hand, the reader must not expect *Under the Net* to manifest all the signs of the later novels; indeed, even the other novels of this early period may be seen as in many ways breaking new ground. For instance, the form of narration is changed: whilst *Under the Net* is told in the first person, the three novels which follow are third-person narratives and it is not until *A Severed Head* that Murdoch again employs a first-person narrator.

The shift of focus in *The Flight from the Enchanter*, *The Sandcastle* and *The Bell* is a shift away from picaresque adventures to a more structured plot and away from what seem to be largely random relationships to more intricate family relationships. In *Under the Net*, it is true, Anna and Sadie are sisters, but their sisterhood is a rather remote bond; 'She's my sister. We put up with each other', remarks Anna (*UTN*, p. 44); the misunderstandings which arise around them have little to do with the two women themselves. Nevertheless, they are the precursors of a line of sororial and fraternal relationships and dependences that stretch throughout the whole gamut of Murdoch's novels and which are generally a starting-point for realisation of the 'otherness' of people, necessary to an understanding of truth and of human values. *The Sandcastle* moves our interest one step further in that for the first time a marital relationship is at the centre of the plot; here it is a marriage that threatens to disintegrate but is saved by the characters being forced to face reality. In

The Bell, on the other hand, Dora and Paul's marriage has already broken down. Again, both the fragility and the resilience of marriage ties are extensively explored in later novels as Murdoch strives to show us that sexual love is no substitute for real spiritual love and that in any relationship there must be a respect for the independence and the 'otherness' of each of the partners.

It is particularly with marital relationships that the next group of novels, to be considered in the following chapter, is concerned, though the comparative simplicity of thought which safeguards the Mors' marriage in *The Sandcastle* on the one hand and on the other hand keeps Paul and Dora apart does not recur. What becomes of compelling and absorbing interest in the later novels is, however, only lightly touched upon in these early novels: the problems of morality, of Good without God, of Good and Evil, of spirituality and redemption which later loom large, are hinted at in *The Bell* but the doubts and agonies which beset the characters in later novels are here kept well beneath the surface.

3

The Romantic Phase

The novels of the 1950s followed each other fairly rapidly, but after *The Bell* there was a three-year gap in publication, the longest gap, in fact, throughout Murdoch's writing career until the gap between her twenty-fourth and twenty-fifth novels, which was, in fact, filled by the publication of her massive philosophical work, *Metaphysics as a Guide to Morals*.

When *A Severed Head* appeared in 1961 it marked some sort of change in which Murdoch seemed to have shifted her ground to look at the moral compulsions which loving entails. This novel, together with *An Unofficial Rose* (1962), *The Unicorn* (1963), *The Italian Girl* (1964) and *The Red and the Green* (1965), represents a romantic phase concerned not only with the philosophic concepts of truth and love which had informed the earlier novels but also and particularly with the responsibilities, impositions and ties of marriage or, in the case of *The Red and the Green*, of religious vocation. Both these problems had been touched on before, though the marital troubles of Mor and his wife in *The Sandcastle* and of Dora and Paul in *The Bell* appeared to be fairly straightforward and the religious difficulties which beset the community at Imber were obsessive only within the actual existence of that community and did not appear to have deeply-rooted superstitions associated with them. What seems to exercise the novelist at this slightly later stage is the terrible strength of inward conditioning, even of secret guilt, arising perhaps from education, from early moral or spiritual guidance or simply from one's own deepest thoughts and reflections.

After his wife has left, Martin Lynch-Gibbon in *A Severed Head* cannot feel he is free; on the contrary he sees himself as in bondage: 'a bond of this kind [i.e. marriage] is deeper and stronger than wanting or not wanting. Wherever I am in the world and whenever I am I shall always be Antonia' (*ASH,* p. 70). In *An Unofficial Rose* Ann, having been deserted by her husband Randall, could perhaps have found happiness with Felix Meecham but at their final encounter Felix feels himself 'destroyed . . . by the sheer overbrimming existence of the absent Randall' (*AUR,* p. 250). In the more enigmatic plot of *The Unicorn* Hannah, though imprisoned in Gaze Castle, is held there mainly by the will of her husband, yet she refuses to be rescued by Pip Lejour and Dennis explains in answer to Marian's question, 'Why not?' that she was 'married to him [i.e. Peter] in church' (*TU,* p. 61). At the end of *The Italian Girl,* when Otto and Isabel part at last, Isabel tells Edmund that she had gone on staying with her husband for so long because, 'I kept being sorry for him in a bad way . . . it was just an obsessive sense of connexion with him . . .' (*TIG,* p. 61).

Whilst marriage is the dark bond in these four novels *The Red and the Green* proposes another kind of bond that Barney Drumm finds himself unable to break – his aborted marriage to the Church. Throughout his 'affair' with Millie and his marriage to Kathleen he has remained physically chaste but nevertheless has endured agonies of guilt at what he sees as a betrayal of his religious vocation:

> He had so much thought himself into the priesthood and he could not now undo this. He was ordained in his mind and his heart and he had no other profession. He was by vocation a failed priest. Yet it was an almost unlivable vocation (*TRATG,* pp. 99f).

There are obvious parallels here with the position of Catherine Fawley in *The Bell*; because of her love for Michael she is about to become by vocation a failed nun and because under such conditions it is an 'unlivable vocation' she tries to kill herself. Likewise, in the same novel, the cycle of separation, reconciliation and renewed separation between Dora and Paul preludes in part the marriage theme of the novels under consideration in this chapter.

It would, however, be simplistic to see these novels as being merely concerned with the unconscious bonds of traditional morality and, indeed, there are ties such as those between Otto and Elsa in *The Italian Girl* or between Hugh Peronett and Emma Sands in *An Unofficial Rose* which defy such a proposition. Yet it is the compulsions, the deeply engrained traditional acceptances, which establish two worlds in the novels – the realistic world of life as it is being lived and the mythical life of the spirit which sees every event as signifying something beyond its apparent meaning, which magnifies the effects of everything that happens and which broods internally, creating monsters in the minds of the protagonists. There is too a deeply disturbing religious undercurrent in these novels. They are about good and evil, about guilt, about sin and redemption, and finally and above all about truth, about understanding the sin in order to achieve the redemption. 'Absolution' wrote Barney Drumm in his memoir, 'requires a definition of sin' (*TRATG*, p. 225); it is the 'definition' of sin and thus, the possibility of absolution, which is so earnestly striven for in this group of novels.

There is, too, an increased interest in narrative methods and in the imposition of outward form upon the novels; all the early novels were divided into chapters but three of the five now under consideration have carefully structured 'Parts' as well and *The Italian Girl* is unique in Murdoch's work in having chapter headings, albeit ironic epigraphs to draw attention to various aspects of the action. Two of the novels, *A Severed Head* and *The Italian Girl* employ a first-person narrator and these illustrate Murdoch's interest in the idea that a person speaks for himself alone, the corollary of this being, once more, that language is an inadequate tool for the understanding of the real world. In the two first-person novels both Martin Lynch-Gibbon and Edmund Narraway give us an entirely solipsistic view of events which precludes the reader from being able at first in any way to assess a wider truth. That there is a truth beyond their simplistic view is, however, fairly quickly evident, at least on a realistic scale. Both narrators are finally, like Jake, forced to understand that they are not at the centre of their world and, further, that what they had seen as the solidity of their world is built upon the quicksands of their own self-deception.

The lies and deceit are underlined in *A Severed Head* by the settings. Though this novel, unlike *The Unicorn*, published two years later, is not set in an isolated spot away from society but is, rather,

set in the heart of London, its characters suffer from acutely claustrophobic surroundings. The plot moves from one closed room to
another, scarcely any event taking place elsewhere. There are only
two outside scenes, the first in Chapter 18 as Martin walks through
mist-shrouded London, the second in the following chapter when
he walks through moonlit Cambridge. In neither of these scenes is
the full light of day allowed to illuminate events. Likewise, when
Martin goes to Liverpool Street Station to meet Honor, though he
is inside, the fog is so thick that 'the great cast-iron dome' of the
station is invisible. In the penultimate chapter we are transported to
London Airport where Martin spends the whole day and where, on
the arrival of Honor, Georgie and Palmer, he attempts to conceal
himself behind an opened newspaper.

The fog of the outside world suggests the miasma which affects
the minds of the characters. The settings may be seen as mirroring
the theatricality of the plot. Detailed descriptions abound, as they
do in the stage directions of the drama of the period, though the
whole story is more like a Restoration comedy than a modern play.
Nevertheless, Murdoch, like (say) Pinter, takes a tight control of
her production, placing the stage props and leaving few of the practical details to our imagination. We might compare her handling of
the background scene in Georgie's room at the opening of the novel
to Pinter's deliberate arranging of his stage in *The Caretaker* (1960);
we must see the shabby inefficiency of Georgie's background in
order, later, to understand Georgie herself and her relationship to
Martin:

> Georgie's room was obscure now except for the light of the
> fire and a trio of red candles burning upon the mantelpiece. The
> candles, together with a few scraggy bits of holly dotted about
> at random, were as near as Georgie, whose 'effects' were always
> a little ramshackle, could get to Christmas decorations, yet the
> room had a glitter all the same as of some half descried treasure
> cavern. In front of the candles, as at an altar, stood one of my
> presents to her, a pair of Chinese incense holders . . . The room
> was heavy with a stifling smell of Kashmir poppy and sandalwood.
> Bright wrapping-paper . . . lay all about, and pushed into a corner
> was the table which still bore the remains of our meal and the
> empty bottle of Château Sancy de Parabère 1955. . . (*ASH*, p. 5).

The emphasis here is on the 'casual' effect of Georgie's arrangements, the 'scraggy' bits of holly, the 'ramshackle' effect, the general untidiness; yet, simultaneously, we have a sense of life, mystery and spirituality brought about by the candles, the incense and the skilfully throwaway simile of the altar; the bottle of wine and the remains of the meal suggest a cosiness and intimacy which Martin never achieves with his wife.

The contrast with Martin's own home is marked. After his encounter with Georgie we find him in Chapter 3 'lying on the big sofa' contemplating his marital drawing-room, which gives off an air of luxurious comfort and suggests a loving care of 'things', a house-pride, a desire to impress that is entirely absent from Georgie's slipshod arrangements:

> A bright fire of coal and wood was glowing and murmuring in the grate, and intermittent lamps lit with a soft gold the long room which, even in winter, by some magic of Antonia's contrived to smell of roses. A large number of expensive Christmas cards were arrayed on the piano; while upon the walls dark evergreens, tied into various clever sprays and joined together by long dropping swags of red and silver ribbon, further proclaimed the season. Antonia's decorations combined a traditional gaiety with the restrained felicity which marked all her domestic arrangements (*ASH*, p. 21).

Nothing is out of place and Martin can luxuriate in its comfort without feeling any sense of reality or of the vivid life which Georgie's room evokes. It has the appearance of a stage setting; it is contrived to exude wealth and good taste but we do not get the impression, as we do in Georgie's room, that Christmas is a happy, carefree family occasion; rather, we feel that presents and Christmas crackers would disturb the elegant balance of the décor and the conviviality of wine and a meal would be unthinkable in this room.

These carefully detailed descriptions are necessary to our understanding of Martin's relationship with the two women, Georgie his mistress and Antonia his wife; they suggest the formal tie which he sees as existing between himself and his wife through their joint possessions and through his appreciation of Antonia's delicately restrained housewifery; they suggest the warmth of his feelings towards

Georgie. As the story moves from one enclosed room to another in a different location, with no apparent interval between, it is like a change of scene in the theatre where we look in upon the action knowing that it is to come to a climax and that the comedy or tragedy must run its course; yet our laughter and our suffering, though vicarious, are real.

Chapter 2, interposed between the contrasting descriptions of the two rooms discussed above, is a reflective one, in which Martin consciously tells the story of his life so far to the reader whom he addresses as 'you'; it is overtly a self-justification of his infidelity to his marriage vows; more covertly it sets in motion the underlying consideration of the nature of truth and love which is the principal theme of the novel. The complications of the plot are constantly prompted by the desire of the characters to break free, not from physical bonds but from those of the mind and spirit: Martin betrays his marriage because of his desire for Georgie who 'was concerned neither with role nor with status' (*ASH*, p. 20); Antonia wants to marry Palmer Anderson because she feels that her present marriage to Martin is 'at a standstill' (*ASH*, p. 26). Yet neither Martin nor Antonia can let go of their marriage and give themselves wholly and unconditionally to another partner; both feel in some way that they are in bondage to tradition; they want to keep what they already have and simply add another layer of relationship. Antonia appears to believe that she and Palmer can hold on to Martin and look after him, despite the separation; Martin himself submits to this at first and, in a desperate effort to hide his own guilt and to put his wife entirely in the wrong, still tries to conceal his clandestine affair with Georgie, even after his marriage has broken down.

The farcical aspects of the plot are used to underline the inability of language to explain adequately the mysteries of human thought and human behaviour, and the fact that they are presented to us through the medium of a fallible and deluded narrator itself adds to the complications. The novel begins with Martin's bold assertion that he is deceiving his wife and as the story progresses it is clear that he is also deceiving Georgie though he is hardly aware of it; the most deceived, however, turns out to be Martin himself: he is doubly deceived by Antonia who leaves him in turn for Palmer and then for Alexander; he is doubly deceived by Georgie who leaves him in turn for Alexander and then for Palmer; he is doubly deceived by both Alexander and Palmer, each of whom takes from him in turn both his wife and his mistress. The novel is essentially a comedy, however, and is to end happily; the very neatness of these infidelities which allow the two women with whom Martin has been involved to find new partners who have also been deeply involved in the plot, leaves the way open for the two remaining actors – Martin and Honor – to come together. These convoluted relationships would have been enough for most novelists without the added complexities of fraternal and sororial involvements but, for reasons discussed in Chapter 1 above, Murdoch repeatedly shows in her novels what almost amounts to an obsession with the idea of brothers and sisters. The somewhat stifling thraldom of such Murdochian relationships was first apparent in *The Flight from the Enchanter*, particularly in the dark mystery of the consanguinity of the Lusiewicz brothers. Here, in *A Severed Head* we find an equally enigmatic relationship between Palmer Anderson and his half-sister Honor Klein, both, like the Lusiewicz brothers, with foreign blood in their veins, Danish-American and German-Jew respectively.

It is not so much the fact of incest between the two, as Martin's discovery of it after his bizarre break-in at Honor's house in the middle of the night, that changes the course of events. His inadvertent voyeurism serves as a catalyst; in discovering his wife's seducer in the act of incest with his own sister, Martin is able to recognise Palmer's Achilles' heel; he finds 'the scales of power inclined in [his] direction' (*ASH*, p. 131) and for the first time in the novel he believes he is able to influence events. He is wrong, of course; alliances re-form without his intervention and the incestuous tie has already been broken by 'the enchantment of untruth' (*ASH*, p. 65) in which Palmer and Antonia are enveloped. At the same time, a strange new tie begins to be formed, for Honor's propensity for myth and fable brings to her mind the classical story of Gyges and Candaules, a story which she persuades Martin to recall on the penultimate page of the book and which encourages and justifies love between her and Martin.

Honor Klein is the principal protagonist of the novel; a Cambridge anthropologist, she has a primitive quality which Georgie recognises at the outset and she broods over the action, constantly demanding that Martin should face up to the truth: 'You cannot cheat the dark gods, Mr Lynch-Gibbon', she asserts when he rejects the proposal that he should fight, metaphorically speaking, for his wife; 'everything in life has to be paid for', she goes on to say, 'and love too has to be paid for' (*ASH*, p. 64). It is she herself who becomes one of the dark gods in the novel, metamorphosing Palmer and Antonia in Martin's imagination into 'deities upon an Indian frieze, enthroned, inhumanly beautiful, a pair of sovereigns' (*ASH*, p. 58); yet, even as he conceives of them thus he sees Honor herself as

> transfigured . . . like some insolent and powerful captain, returning booted and spurred from a field of triumph . . . confronting the sovereign powers whom he was now ready if need be to bend to his will (*ASH*, p. 58).

First Palmer and then Martin are enslaved by her and perhaps the price that has to be paid for her is that of 'defining the sin', facing up to the dark gods and seeing through the tangle of untruth the glimmerings of reality. Palmer fails the test: he believes himself to be in love with Antonia but cannot relinquish Honor and thus loses them both; we cannot know if Georgie is a satisfactory substitute.

A. S. Byatt in her British Council booklet, *Iris Murdoch*,[1] describes the central image of the severed head as the 'image of the petrifying Medusa' but, towards the end of the novel, Honor sees herself as a severed head 'such as primitive tribes . . . used to use' believing that with a morsel of gold on its tongue it could utter prophecies. The prophecies she utters at the time suggest no future for love between her and Martin but despite this he feels that 'she had, effectively, given me hope; and she was no fool' (*ASH*, p. 185). Antonia, too, is a severed head – the bronze sculpted head that Alexander had made of her years before. When Martin comments that a sculpted head seems to him to represent 'an illicit and incomplete relationship' (*ASH*, p. 44), he little realises that Alexander is later to perfect that relationship by claiming Antonia for himself.

When at the end Martin believes that he has lost everything as he sees the passengers depart for America, he returns to his flat in Lowndes Square. Suddenly, for the first time in the novel, the scene is illuminated; he turns on all the lights and as he prepares to draw the curtains he is able to see outside where the trees are lit up by the street lamps and the lights of cars can be seen 'in endless procession'. The darkness and the gloomy interiors of the rest of the

book have given way to clarity and brightness, which prepare the
reader for the final scene in which Martin and Honor come together at last, the insincerity and untruths vanquished by the shining light of a triumphant love.

The mythic element of the novel is reinforced once more by its
theatricality. In his article 'Iris Murdoch: Everybody through the
Looking-Glass',[2] Leonard Kriegel makes much of the idea that
Murdoch 'fails to establish true credibility for her characters'; the
title of the piece intends to convey what he sees as the unreality of
Murdoch's world, more like that of Lewis Carroll than of the world
we live in. He has not, however, recognised the deliberate staging
of the action of the novels, the dual plot, the mythological story
which runs parallel with the story of the real world and which is
necessary to an understanding of that real world. At the end of *A
Severed Head* Martin considers his present in the light of the events
of the past weeks. The pain he is suffering is real: 'the sharp truth
would not be denied and I . . . became myself in the knowledge of
my unique loss' (*ASH*, p. 202). From a position outside himself he
looks upon his role as husband, his role as betrayer of his marriage,
his role as cuckold and recognises that they were only parts he was
playing. Now the play is over and he is no more and no less than
his own real self. Looking back as at a dream he knows that, 'There
had been a drama, there had been some characters, but now everyone else was dead and only in me a memory remained of what had
been' (*ASH*, p. 201).

Meanwhile, we can now see him stripped of pretensions, all the
false roles behind him; almost throughout, we have been aware that
his own solipsistic view of himself has been an act which we, together
with the other members of the cast, have been watching with interest. This kind of simultaneous duality of action is often present in
Shakespearean drama when the theatre audience find themselves
observing not only the main action of the play but also a group of
characters who have become part of a 'subtext' within the play.
Such is the eavesdropping scene in *Twelfth Night*, when Sir Toby
and his accomplices gull Malvolio whilst the audience watch Malvolio
the Player and at the same time watch the play's internal audience
who become both players and spectators. Similarly, in *A Midsummer Night's Dream*, the action in the woods is regarded with what
Hermia calls, a 'parted eye,/When everything seems double' and

Demetrius questions whether he is yet awake: 'It seems to me/That yet we sleep, we dream'.

Indeed, *A Severed Head* in its complexities of romantic attachments has some affinity with Shakespeare's romantic comedies, particularly the two mentioned above, and Murdoch, like Shakespeare in *Twelfth Night*, seems to be mocking the whole concept of romance. The whirligig of time has spun all the main characters through different relationships until at the end pairing seems to be finally resolved and Martin looks to the hope of coming with Honor 'through the dream and out into the waking world' (*ASH*, p. 205).

A Severed Head and the following novel, *An Unofficial Rose*, are the only ones of the period of the early 1960s in which the violence of death does not occur, though here physical violence is present in Georgie's attempted suicide, in the fight between Martin and Honor and in Martin's attack upon Palmer; in *An Unofficial Rose* it is mainly violence or violation of the spirit which occurs, for instance, in the quarrel between Randall and Ann in Chapter 6, or in the breaking of Penn by Miranda in Chapter 29. The romantic situations in this novel are far less comic than those in the preceding novel, partly because they are less complicated and thus less like a bedroom farce. The emphasis is upon the cyclic nature of life, in which Hugh, albeit almost unwillingly, conspires to allow his son Randall to fulfil in his life the romantic episode which Hugh himself as a young man had allowed to escape him. Randall is quick to seize the moment and the money and leave with Lindsay Rimmer for Rome, where he enjoys waking ecstasy but at night suffers disturbed dreams in which he returns again and again to his marital home only to find that the presence of his wife eludes him. Like Rupert Brooke sitting in a café in Berlin writing 'The Old Vicarage, Grantchester' Randall, from his Italian love-nest looks back with an emotion almost like regret at his 'unofficial rose', Ann, his deserted wife, at home in England. The melancholy ending in which romance is thwarted, at least for Ann and Felix, leaves them to accept their loss and reshape their lives; for Hugh, however, who has lost Emma, there appears to be the possibility of a final fling with Mildred Finch.

The Unicorn, like *The Bell*, is set in an enclosed community, that of Gaze Castle which, though the novel does not actually say so, appears to be in Ireland. It is the first of two novels in this group to be set in Ireland. Unlike Imber Court, however, Gaze holds its inhabitants captive and escape appears to be impossible until the spell is broken. When Marian Taylor arrives as 'governess' and first views the house she feels immediate terror; the Gothic quality of the surroundings impinge themselves graphically upon her mind:

> The car bumped over a jangling cattle-grid and through an immense crenellated archway. A lodge cottage with blank gaping windows and a sagging roof stood in a wilderness of wind-torn shrubs. The uneven gravel track, devastated by rain and weeds, wound away to the left, circling upward toward the house (*TU*, p. 16).

Once inside Gaze Castle itself her feeling of fear intensifies:

> The floors were mostly uncarpeted, tilting, creaking, echoing, but there were soft hangings above her head, curtains in archways and vague cobwebby textiles which hung down at doors and corners and tugged her passing sleeve (*TU*, p. 17).

and, at the end of the first chapter, the sense that she is being watched through the binoculars of an unknown man in Riders, the house across the valley, renews her panic.

Iris Murdoch herself has stated quite clearly, 'I would not like to be labelled as a Gothic novelist' (*Rencontres*, p. 85) and I think that we cannot see this novel as truly 'Gothic' except in its setting. Marian, who is moved by an undefined fear at the beginning does not let fantasy run away with her; rather, she brings reason to bear upon the problems that face her at Gaze. What she does not understand is the spiritual dimension of Hannah's captivity. The Gothic elements serve the same purpose as the theatrical elements of so many of the novels – they enable us to look in upon the story from outside, whilst we simultaneously empathise with the characters.

Though she is the principal consciousness of the novel, Marian is not the main protagonist; like Rain in *The Sandcastle* or Dora in *The Bell*, she is the outsider, the catalyst who changes and finally destroys life at Gaze. Assisting her in this task is Effingham Cooper, also an outsider and the other character through whose consciousness we see the events as they pass. Both Marian and Effie have to learn of the past piecemeal and as they learn of Hannah's imprisonment

– through Jamesie and Denis and Pip – we too are able to piece
the story together. Again it is a story on more than one level and
the somewhat bizarre surface story is necessary to the mythological and theatrical stories that lie beneath.

The themes of the novel, like those of Tennyson's 'The Lady of
Shalott', are of loss and desire, of appearance and reality, of love
and truth and, like the Lady in the poem, Hannah appears to be
enchanted and to have a curse upon her if she attempts to leave her
prison. She lives in a world of shadows, for the people around her
no longer seem to have reality in relation to her but are playing
their parts in a drama that has to be played out to its conclusion.
Early on in the novel it becomes evident that the old magic number
seven has acquired mythological significance (and we might remember
here that *The Unicorn* is Murdoch's seventh novel): seven years
before the story begins, Hannah had apparently tried (unsuccess-
fully) to kill her husband, Peter; he has been absent for seven years;
Hannah has been imprisoned for seven years. 'Why seven years?'
Marian asks Denis and answers her own question, 'Just because
that's the time things go on for in fairy tales?' (*TU*, p. 64) but the
very positing of the question serves to feed the myth; Marian is
aware that she has come to Gaze at the end of the seven years and
she becomes obsessed with slotting herself into the plot, for she is
convinced that everything in the tale is predetermined and that nothing
can be seen as a random event; Marian's reality becomes subsumed
into the fairy story so that she is both part of the plot and simultaneously an onlooker at the play unfolding around and before her.

As so often in Murdoch's novels, the vocabulary constantly draws
attention to the theatrical elements of the story; we have seen how
the Gothic elements serve as a setting for the whole plot, but in
Chapter 6, for example, Marian feels as if she and Hannah are on a
stage and the 'sense of play-acting' makes her see Hannah as if she
were 'some brave beleaguered lady in a legend' (*TU*, p. 50), indeed
perhaps, as I have suggested above, a Lady of Shalott. By the end
of the chapter Marian too appears to be bewitched and held captive; certainly she is prevented from going out of the garden, first
by the sheer physical resistance of the gate but also, more ominously, by a psychological fear that holds her back and makes her
afraid to go outside; so she remains, a character on a stage defined
by the bounds of Gaze Castle, forced to take part in the drama that

is unfolding and watched by the grass on the cliff 'cold and attentive, visible yet unreal, waiting to see what she would do' (*TU*, p. 55).

Max Lejour emphasises the duality of the story in his philosophical discussion with Effingham in Chapter 12 when he equates Hannah with a scapegoat, a term irrevocably linked with the suffering Christ. 'She is our image of the significance of suffering', he comments, 'But we must also see her as real. And that will make us suffer too'. The very title of the novel demands a mixed reaction, the snow-white unicorn of myth having been associated in iconography with both Christ and the Virgin Mary. So Hannah is both mythological character, through whom we learn a moral lesson and, simultaneously, real human being in whose suffering we vicariously share. If we insist on seeing her only on the level of myth, then the story becomes unreal, merely a metaphor; when we view her as also flesh and blood, as one of ourselves, then our hearts become involved. For Max, the story of Hannah is inextricably linked with the concept of truth and thus with expiation and redemption; freedom he sees, echoing Jake's words in *Under the Net*, as 'a flimsy idea' (*TU*, p. 97), not as a cure for the ills of oppression, for 'in morals we are all prisoners' and to break out of the inhibitions which surround us does not take us closer to truth. When, at the end, Max becomes Hannah's material heir, he dispels the romantic aura which surrounded Hannah and everyone is forced to face their moment of truth. Jamesie sees that the 'play is over' (*TU*, p. 253) and takes Violet away; Denis explains to Marian that 'the spell is broken and the magic is all blown away' (*TU*, p. 259); Effingham tells Alice that 'this adventure is over for me, and you, through having become a part of it, are over too' (*TU*, p. 266).

Whilst in *A Severed Head* the love complications are seen as comic, in this novel they have the potential for tragedy. Hannah, who has broken her marriage vows to her husband Peter by accepting Pip Lejour as her lover, has brought a terrible vengeance down upon herself but in her enigmatic position as a prisoner she becomes a romantic focus for the other actors in the drama. Legends of imprisoned ladies and their knights play upon their minds but it is not easy to rescue a princess who does not desire rescue. Like the Lady of Shalott, only she can effect the breaking of the spell (Marian actually describes this as 'want[ing] to break the mirror') (*TU*, p. 247) and thus choose her own destiny.

The violence of multiple deaths brings the plot to its close: Gerald is shot by Hannah; Peter is deliberately drowned by Denis; Hannah and her one-time lover Pip both kill themselves. As in a Shakespearean tragedy, however, myth and magic are dispersed and the forces of normality prevail at the end: Gaze Castle will soon be left empty; Denis leaves, having confessed to Marian that he killed Peter; life resumes at Riders; Marian prepares to go back 'to the real world' (*TU*, p. 264) and Effingham, too, tells Alice that they must 'return to our real life and our real tasks' (*TU*, p. 266).

As in *The Bell* there is an overtly religious theme in this novel and Hannah, like Catherine, is the tainted postulant. As a recluse, she is living through her guilt which is finally atoned for in her death. Denis Nolan sees her as entrapped by her own sin, unable to escape; at the same time she is for him a sort of Christ-figure, expiating the sins of the world:

> The soul under the burden of sin cannot flee. What is enacted here with her is enacted with all of us in one way or another. You cannot come between her and her suffering, it is too complicated, too precious. . . . she has made her peace with God (*TU*, pp. 65–6).

After her death and the murder of Peter, it is Denis who becomes the scapegoat and who metaphorically goes out into the wilderness with his burden of guilt upon him.

The Unicorn was followed by what is probably the least successful of all Murdoch's novels, *The Italian Girl*. I believe that this lack of success is mainly because the mythical and realistic elements are insufficiently fused, with the consequence that even Edmund Narraway, the first-person narrator, is unconvincing. Like *An Unofficial Rose*, it begins with a family bereavement and, though Fanny Peronett and Lydia Narraway were very different in character, their deaths appear to release their families from normal social inhibitions. The problem for the reader of the later novel is that the characters remain mythological and the ending is like that of a fairy tale as Edmund evokes the magical Italian names: 'Genova, Pisa, Livorno, Grosseto, Civitavecchia, Roma . . .'.

The Red and the Green (1965) is ostensibly a new departure for Murdoch. Set in Ireland in the troubles of Easter 1916, it is a carefully researched historical romance. In *Rencontres* Murdoch explained that:

> For that particular week [the week of the 1916 rebellion which the novel is about] I tried to get everything right – what day a particular article was published on, what day and how they changed the plan for the insurrection, and what the English were doing, what everybody was doing during that week (*Rencontres*, p. 92).

Within its historical framework, however, the novel has much in common with the other four novels I have grouped with it for, despite the excitements and terrors of the Rising, the principal interest is a romantic one.

The family relationships here are at their most complicated in the novels so far because the whole *dramatis personae* – mothers, fathers, sons, daughters, brothers, cousins, aunts, uncles, the Chase-Whites, the Dumays, the Drumms, the Kinnards and the Bellmans – all belong to several generations of one large extended Anglo-Irish family, with its complications of intermarriage, its confused allegiances to Britain and Ireland and its shifting attachments to Protestantism and Catholicism. Yet the very choice of such a family to people the historical event illustrates the dilemma of Ireland. The traditional compulsions which in earlier novels had centred on the commitments and responsibilities of marriage are here linked to nationalism and to religion, though the novel is less successful in making its readers believe in the depth of emotion that ties Pat Dumay to Ireland and to Catholicism than in convincing us of his deep affection for his younger brother Cathal.

The twist of fortune which has made Andrew Chase-White feel himself 'unreflectively to be English', yet normally to describe himself 'equally unreflectively' as Irish (TRATG, p. 8) has also brought it about that he has become a serving officer in the British Army whilst his Irish cousins are plotting insurrection against the British. Furthermore, his not quite formalised engagement to his cousin Frances is part of a pattern of unfulfilled love entanglements that pervade the book, with Millie Kinnard overtly at the centre.

Millie is a destructive force; she flirts with the menfolk of both

generations, destroying first Barney Drumm's vocation and then his
marriage to her sister-in-law, Kathleen; whilst keeping Barney as
her 'dear old sheepdog' (*TRATG*, p. 126), she accepts Christopher
Bellman's proposal of marriage; simultaneously, she takes away
Andrew's virginity and lusts after Pat Dumay, Barney's stepson.
Millie is essentially evil and the suffering she inflicts is not merely
emotional, for both Barney and Andrew, in their different ways,
have their lives ruined by her. Barney's special attraction for her
was his dedication to the priesthood, his feeling that his body was
'a pure vessel, a spiritual temple, scoured, empty and awaiting the
final installation of a ghostly visitor' (*TRATG*, p. 93). It was not
possible for him, however, to become a priest and to love Millie
and once he had become a spoiled priest, 'stripped of his soutane, a
miserable confused young man' (*TRATG*, p. 94), Millie ceased to
take any interest in 'him.

Barney Drumm, above all the other characters, epitomises the
muddle of Ireland; born a Protestant and brought up in London, he
converts to Catholicism and begins to train for the priesthood. Corrupted by the ungodly Millie and thus unable to fulfil his religious
vocation, he links himself in marriage to the devout Catholic Kathleen,
the widow of Millie's brother Brian and brings up Brian's two revol-
utionary sons, Pat and Cathal, by whom, despite his background
and the mildness of his temperament, he is persuaded to throw in
his lot with the Irish Volunteer Army. Though Millie constantly
rejects him and though he feels inescapably bound by his Catholic
marriage, he clings to the idea that he and Millie are also in some
way bound to each other. He is a man of many contradictions who
would have 'been a vegetarian if it wasn't for his passion for saus-
ages' (*TRATG*, p. 278). It is typical of him that on the fateful morning
of Easter Monday 1916 as he goes off to fight with the rebels he
accidentally, though not merely metaphorically, shoots himself in
the foot and is unable to go on. Barney finds an illusory freedom
in writing his memoir but it is a freedom based on fantasy; his
Memoir serves as a justification for his life:

There had to be somewhere . . . where he was justified and
[Kathleen] was judged. In real life she was all judge, even when
she said nothing. In the Memoir everything was reversed and the
unfairness of life was done away with and that dreadful power

was quenched .... . What he wrote in the Memoir was not quite true, and that 'not quite' was the stuff of a most wicked lie (*TRATG*, p. 175).

Unlike Martin Lynch-Gibbon in *A Severed Head*, Barney Drumm is aware of reality but he chooses to ignore it, preferring his own interpretation of his life because that is less harrowing. Even after his Lenten decision to destroy the Memoir he makes excuses to himself until the moment that he agrees to fight on the side of the rebels. His *alter ego* of the Memoir then becomes superfluous and he tears it up.

If Millie is at one end of the moral spectrum and Barney indeterminately in the middle, Pat Dumay is at the other end. Loved by Millie, by Frances and by his cousin Andrew he is not corrupted by them. For him love is real; his love for his brother Cathal and his love for Ireland are weighed in the balance and only his own honour seems able to tip it towards Ireland. He alone of the characters in the novel dies in the Uprising.

The historical dimension of the novel serves to some extent to obscure its moral and philosophical aspects, particularly as the political issues are not presented in terms of black and white. At the same time, the historicity is muted and the novel proper ends before the climax of battle takes place, thus emphasising that it is about people, not events.

Aesthetically the 'Epilogue' is unsatisfactory. It is placed chronologically, by the dating of Kathleen's letter to Frances, twenty-two years after the main events of the novel. Its deliberate intention is to tie together all the loose ends. Murdoch was very aware of her own propensity to make a neatly complete ending to her novels:

I think this is always a temptation that a novelist has (particularly a novelist like myself who is interested in plots and patterns), that he must relate everybody to everybody. . . . Novelists must resist the temptation to tie up all the loose ends (*Rencontres*, p. 74).

Kathleen's letter is reinforced by the questions of Frances's English family, her husband and her 'tall son', who is like Cathal. Most of the violence of the novel is distanced by being contained within this Epilogue, particularly the deaths of all the men of the younger generation, Pat and Cathal Dumay and Andrew Chase-White. Furthermore, it once more brings into play Murdoch's interest in cyclical events. Frances's son not only looks like Cathal, he is almost a reincarnation of Cathal, and Frances's present fear is that he will follow his best friend who has joined the International Brigade and gone to fight in the Spanish Civil War. The romantic note with which the novel ends – Frances's confession that she was in love with Pat Dumay – adds a slightly new perspective to the plot but it appears to be an unimportant and unsatisfactory embroidery of what turns out to be a not-entirely-convincing novel. Unlike the revelations which make Jake Donoghue revise his understanding of all the relationships in the novel and which thus reinterpret the events of the plot for us, Frances's declaration of her love in no way alters the basic story, though retrospectively it perhaps explains her reluctance to become formally engaged to Andrew. The problem is that we find it a little difficult to see her avowal as sincere and are therefore unwilling to accept it as an explanation. The revelation is aimed merely at the reader; it is our view of things that is intended to be changed, not that of any of the actors in the drama.

Though I have categorised these five novels as 'romantic' they are novels which enlarge the view of violence that was apparent in the earlier group; here violence is seen to be not only a physical but also a moral violation. *An Unofficial Rose* and *The Unicorn* are particularly disturbing in their depiction of psychological subjugation. Evil too is depicted more graphically in these novels than in the earlier ones. The 'dark gods' of *A Severed Head* are finally, it would seem, merely mischievous, but palpable evil is apparent in all of the other four novels, through Miranda in *An Unofficial Rose*, through Gerald and the absent Peter in *The Unicorn*, through the mischievous and sensuous David Levkin in *The Italian Girl* and through his female counterpart, Millie, in *The Red and the Green*.

The next group of novels expands on these themes and examines more seriously good and evil in conflict.

4
Conflicts of Good and Evil

The Time of the Angels (1966), the novel which follows *The Red and the Green*, sets a more sombre tone than most of its predecessors, with the possible exception of *The Unicorn*. The group of novels which it introduces – *The Nice and the Good* (1968), *Bruno's Dream* (1969), A *Fairly Honourable Defeat* (1970) and *An Accidental Man* (1971) – though still funny, often farcical, are deeply concerned with the problems of Good and Evil. At times they are infused with a palpable, almost demonic evil, coupled with a negation of the existence of God.

If one does not believe in a personal God there is no problem of evil, but there is the almost insuperable difficulty of looking properly at evil and human suffering

Murdoch commented in 1969, in the essay 'On "God" and "Good"'.[1]

It is with this concept that she seems to struggle in the group of novels now under consideration. In contradistinction to William Golding's view of evil as indigenous to Man, Iris Murdoch appears in this group of novels to view evil as stemming from catalytic figures who destroy the peace and tranquillity of the world around them. She sees existential man as descending from Kantian man: 'Kant', she explains, 'abolished God and made man God in his stead . . . this man is with us still, free, independent, lonely, powerful, rational,

55

responsible, brave . . . his proper name is Lucifer' (*SOG*, pp. 79–
80). It is just such a man who is placed at the centre of several of
the novels of this period, the hero who seeks to undermine the simpler characters by testing the quality of their 'goodness', whose sense
of power is manifested by his own self-regard and his apparent in-
difference to those around him.

Though Murdoch sees the novel in general as 'a comic form' and
claims that her own books are 'full of happiness', she is also aware
of the magnetism of evil:

> one tends to be impressed by the people who are demonic. . . . I
> think one identifies with the demonic characters in books, since
> it's a deep notion to feel that the devil tempts you and gives you
> power in return for giving up goodness, which is after all often
> dull (Haffenden, p. 204).

Thus, Carel Fisher in *The Time of the Angels* or Julius King in *A
Fairly Honourable Defeat* impose themselves upon our minds much
more forcibly than do their 'good' counterparts, Eugene Peshkov,
Rupert Foster and Tallis Browne.

If any one of Murdoch's novels can be seen as not 'full of happiness', it is *The Time of the Angels* which, despite its often farcical
humour, is a somewhat depressing novel. Superficially, like *The
Unicorn*, it again contains Gothic elements. The opening pages, setting the scene in the cold and gloomy rectory, have overtones of
Gothic horror with their references to the dark, the cold, the fog
and the noise of the underground railway reverberating through the
house. As Pattie prepares to light the fire Gothic images abound:
the cinders she piles on top of the sticks are 'rusty' and 'misshapen';
the lighted match illuminates 'a picture of some black men tortur-
ing some other black men' and the fire crackles into a blazing in-
ferno. There is talk of saving spiders from death and catching mice
in traps and over it all, concealed by the darkness, hovers the black-
cassocked rector, avoiding any possible contact with the outside world.

Though he speaks the first word in the book, Carel Fisher, the
Rector, appears to lack ordinary human identity; to begin with he is
just a voice and whenever he is present his person is obscure. In
contradiction of his holy calling, Carel is identified with darkness;

he is a mysterious and sinister figure who, though he is the central character of the novel, is extremely elusive. At the same time he is the unifying force behind the *dramatis personae*. He is related to several of the other characters – he is the brother of Marcus, the father of Muriel and also, as it turns out, of Elizabeth, though his putative role in regard to her is that of uncle and guardian. The servant Pattie is his mistress, as also is Elizabeth with whom his relationships are multiple and complex. Anthea Barlow had once been in love with him, and perhaps, we may assume from her tears at the end of the novel, still is. Eugene Peshkov and his son have their own quarters in the Rectory, where Eugene acts as 'porter'. The Rectory itself, in which most of the action takes place, is Carel's by right of his job, a job which is essentially a sinecure, since except for its tower the church has been destroyed, the church hall is not consecrated and in Norah Shadox-Brown's words, 'The Rector can do as much or as little as he pleases. . . . It's obviously a niche for problem children' (*TOA*, p. 13).

Carel's problem, as a minister of the Church, is that he does not believe in the existence of God. He foreshadows a number of priestly figures who appear in later novels and who have lost their faith; unlike Carel, however, most of them continue to struggle with the concept of goodness. In particular we should note how Father Bernard the Catholic priest in *The Philosopher's Pupil*, in discussion with the philosopher Rozanov, refers to 'the problem of our age, our interregnum, our interim, our time of the angels' and, asked why he talked of angels, he explains 'Spirit without God' (*PP*, p. 188).

Carel Fisher justifies his position, however, by asserting that 'If there is no God there is all the more need for a priest' (*TOA*, p. 79). Nevertheless, he is not free of God; rather, he is obsessed by the 'God-myth'. When he talks of the death of God he does not appear to view God as non-existent from eternity to eternity; he sees him in some way as having existed and existing no more, as though Lucifer's fallen angels had won their battle and set unredeemed evil loose in the world, as though, perhaps, he is himself one of the fallen angels, the 'lapsed soul' of Blake's poem which has for Pattie 'taken the place of . . . prayer' (*TOA*, p. 10). Carel has recreated God in his own image and substituted self 'for the true object of veneration' (*SOG*, p. 101): 'When I celebrate mass', he tells Marcus, 'I am God' (*TOA*, p. 174), yet as far as Carel takes on any identity, it is a demonic one; he is the dark opposite to goodness, to morality, a god of the underworld. For Muriel, 'There had always been an area of darkness in her relationship with her father' (*TOA*, p. 179); she sees Eugene Peshkov as 'an essential counterweight to Carel, the white figure against the black one' (*TOA*, p. 179). Yet, despite the evil that Carel appears to represent, he is a focus of love. Pattie loves him completely, absolutely and desperately; she will put up with almost any indignity for his sake; when he takes her as his mistress she surrenders to him blindly; when he ceases to visit her bed she accepts the change despairingly. After his final encounter with him, Marcus finds himself 'in a condition which could only be described as being in love with Carel' (*TOA*, p. 192). And as she lets him die, Muriel knows that she 'loved her father and she had loved him only' (*TOA*, p. 221). Love, however, we should remember, does not reflect the quality of the loved but is, rather, an attribute of the one who loves: in 'The Sovereignty of Good Over Other Concepts'[2] Murdoch remarks that love is 'capable of infinite degradation' but that it may also be 'the force that joins us to Good' (*SOG*, p. 103).

The thought that, like Faustus, Carel has sold his soul to the devil is inescapable. An echo from Marlowe's *Faustus* in the third chapter connects the two stories and already prepares us for Carel's death: 'Lo where Christ's blood streamed in the firmament' (*TOA*, p. 26). In his compact with Lucifer, Faustus chose to gratify his own desires and abjure God. Carel too has rejected redemption, for in rejecting God he has also rejected Good, a concept which should move outward towards others, rather than inward towards oneself. In the creation of his own godhead he has imposed a moral and spiritual tyranny upon those whose lives in some way depend upon him and, in turn, he takes upon himself their 'creation' – Muriel and Elizabeth, his children in the flesh; Marcus, whom he makes 'exist . . . just for a moment' (*TOA*, p. 176) and Pattie, whom he created 'a goddess' (*TOA*, p. 27) and whom, later, 'fumbling . . . to undo the front of her blouse' he attempts to recreate as a Black Virgin Mary: 'Hail Pattie, full of grace, the Lord is with thee, blessed art thou among women' (*TOA*, p. 158).

Faustus, when he knew that the end of his allotted time on earth was approaching, believed that supernatural powers were lying in wait for him; likewise, Carel sees rats and mice and 'a black thing' manifesting themselves in his presence, though Pattie knows that 'what frightened Carel did not belong to the material world' (*TOA*, p. 32). The idea of demonic possession is presented to us through her; completely subservient to Carel, she slowly realises that something is happening inside his mind:

> Pattie apprehended at last something like a great fear in Carel, a fear which afflicted her with terror and with a kind of nausea. It seemed to her now that . . . she had always seen him as a soul in hell. Carel was becoming very frightened and he carried fear about with him as a physical environment (*TOA*, p. 32).

Carel himself, in fact, scarcely seems to belong to the material world. He belongs inside the Rectory, which is his prison, his Gaze Castle and inside the Rectory he imprisons Elizabeth by an act of will similar to that which holds Hannah at Gaze; neither he nor Elizabeth ever goes outside the doors and no one from outside is allowed in; when others from inside – Pattie, Muriel, Leo – go out, they are generally enveloped in fog which conceals the identity of the Rectory; likewise, when anyone from outside manages to enter, as does Marcus, Carel's identity is concealed by an impenetrable darkness. The comedy which develops in the dark and fog of *A Severed Head*, however, here turns to tragedy but, just as the earlier novel ends in a blaze of light, so in this novel, the fog lifts after Carel's death; 'fallen, fallen light'[3] is renewed; Muriel pulls the curtains back and she sees 'a little blue sky and the sun [is] shining' (*TOA*, p. 222). In her philosophical writings Murdoch often refers to Plato's idea that the good man, after various vicissitudes, is eventually able to emerge from the Cave and to look at the sun: 'The sun', she explains, 'represents the Form of the Good in whose light the truth is seen; it reveals the world, hitherto invisible, and is also a source of life'.[4] Earlier, in her essay 'On "God" and "Good"' she had commented, 'What does seem to make perfect sense in the Platonic myth is the idea of the Good as the source of light which reveals to us all things as they really are' (*SOG*, p. 70).

The metaphorical significance of darkness may thus be seen in Murdoch's novels to represent an absence of Good, breeding a secrecy which obscures reality. That Carel is never able to face the light of day must suggest his opposition, his hostility to Good. In Chapter

14 when there is a brief lifting of the fog and the darkness, there is
a simultaneous lightening of the atmosphere: Eugene and Pattie go
out together from the Rectory and the action is transposed to the
sparkling outdoors, as though they have escaped from the Cave.
For the first time in the novel there is a pervading sense of happiness:

> The huge echoing light, the dense feel of the stone, the hasten-
> ing movement of the wide river, the glittering arc of buildings
> low upon the horizon, dazed and transported [Eugene]. He felt
> himself the centre of some pure transparent system, infinitely
> spinning, infinitely still. There was no place in this limpid uni-
> verse where darkness could hide. He said, 'Pattie, I feel so full
> of joy, I hardly know where I am' (*TOA*, p. 147).

There follows the declaration of love between them. The unalloyed
joy of being able to look at the sun suggests the true goodness of
Eugene, the goodness which subdues self and makes one look outward towards others. He offers Pattie a selfless love (an important
criterion for Plato in understanding the principle of Good), which
makes no demands on her and a 'moral' love through marriage
which is briefly able to restore her self-respect.

The chapter which follows illustrates the reversal of Plato's proposal and the depth of Carel's corruption. The sun still shines and
its hope still suffuses through Pattie; what she has always longed
for is to 'be married, to be ordinary, to love in innocence' yet when
she contemplates Eugene's offer she realises that, though it is 'perfectly possible', it is also 'totally impossible' (*TOA*, p. 154). This
thought is followed immediately by the entrance of Carel, wearing
dark glasses to obscure the sun and demanding that the curtains
should be pulled across so that he is protected from the glare. The
catechism of love which follows (an irreverent parody of the Catechism from the Prayer Book) contrasts with the love scene of the
previous chapter. Here, once again, Carel hijacks the God-myth,
demanding of Pattie a love which is willing to be crucified for him
and, as though he has some demonic knowledge of Eugene's proposal and is determined to thwart it, the chapter ends in a blasphemous
copulation.

Yet Pattie, despite Carel's efforts to win her to evil, finally escapes. Torn between the good Eugene and the corrupt Carel, she

submits at first to the seductions of evil, because she mistakes them for genuine love. Carel is to her what he is to himself – God. When she first went to work for Carel at the country rectory:

> She entered into Carel's presence as into the presence of God, and like the souls of the blessed, realized her felicity ... by a sense of her own body as glorified. . . . Carel's divine hands created her in her turn a goddess . . . (*TOA*, p. 27).

Thirteen years later Pattie still clings to her uncritical love for the Rector, 'He was the Lord God and she was the inert and silent earth which moves in perfect obedience' (*TOA*, p. 208), but when she learns of his incestuous relationship with Elizabeth, her spirit deserts him:

> She would have to go, she would have to leave him at last. She loved him, but she could do nothing with her love. It was for her own torment only and not for his salvation. She did not love him enough to save him ... She could not make his miracle of redemption (*TOA*, p. 212).

Though it is too late to save her love with Eugene, it is not too late for Pattie to save herself and she escapes from the Rectory to work in an African refugee camp, fulfilling her secret dream of dedicating herself 'to the service of humanity and [being] Patricia for ever and ever after' (*TOA*, pp. 31–2).

The Time of the Angels is a novel which plays with philosophical concepts that were very much to the forefront of Murdoch's mind at the time of writing it. It may perhaps be seen as a dramatic presentation of some of the ideas which later appeared in *The Sovereignty of Good*, particularly in the essay 'On "God" and "Good"', first published in 1969 three years after the publication of *The Time of the Angels*. The principal concept in Marcus's projected book, *Morality in a World without God* is constantly present in the novel itself; like Murdoch, he is willing to dispense with God but he is made anxious by the thought of a system of a 'morality without Good' (*TOA*, p. 71) and this worry pervades the novel as an undercurrent, disturbing our pure pleasure at the novel's comedy and underlining our anxiety about its central moral concepts. As Marcus struggles to establish 'the idea of an Absolute in morals', however, he finds that the thread of his argument has become lost in his overwhelming concern about Carel and Elizabeth.

Running parallel to the contemplation of philosophic thought in the novel is the actual action, which is deeply concerned with ideas of Good and Evil as they are manifested in man and with the existence or non-existence of God. On a lower plane, Leo and Muriel discuss the question of morals and seem at first bent on outdoing each other in their declarations of their own immorality; yet at the end of the discussion they make a comic parody of genuine religious rites: Leo is persuaded by Muriel to make a sacrifice to the Thames to atone for the lies he has told about his father and he throws his college scarf into the water; Muriel, who has also lied, has to expiate her wrongdoing with a kiss. Again and again serious moral argument is undermined by the black comedy of events: Marcus's first interview with Carel when he enters the Rectory through the coal-hole ends with the Rector's obscene jest in which he places the carrot-penis in his brother's hand; the prologue to the second interview is the bedroom farce which finds Leo and Muriel struggling together in the linen cupboard and which ends in Muriel's voyeuristic view of the incestuous copulation of Carel and Elizabeth. These ideas cannot be ignored, for they obtrude upon any interpretation of character, they puzzle, they leave us bewildered as to what message, if any, is the final one of the novel.

In other ways, however, this novel has much in common with those that preceded it. The theatricality and the comedy are still present, though considerably toned down and overlaid with the sense of mystery, even of fear. There are fewer elaborate scenes of spectacle but they are certainly still present and Carel himself has a superb sense of the theatrical. His role as the priest of no-God sets him constantly at centre-stage – a voice, a dark presence at the top of the stairs, a half-illuminated face and then, through the spy-hole in the linen-cupboard, a head and naked torso, the defrocked priest performing his primitive rites. The claustrophobia of the earlier novels is here almost suffocating as the reader's attention is closely focused on these staged episodes, to the exclusion of the outside world.

Murdoch's enjoyment of the detailed descriptions of intricate mechanisms for achieving particular ends is less evident than it was in the theft of Mr Mars in *Under the Net* but, had the scene not been enacted in complete darkness, Marcus's entry into the Rectory through the coal-hole would be visually just as funny. His descent, however, is a metaphorical fall into the pit of hell and his comic emergence from darkness into an even more palpable darkness, to be confronted by the invisible incarnation of the devil himself, is comprehended on two levels at once: the farcical event in the realm of reality and the insubstantial event in the metaphysical world of the spirit. We are constantly suspended between these two worlds, unsure of the demarcation line between the tangible and what lies beyond, between the ordered and the chaotic. There is a confusing plurality of character and of action which, at the end of the novel dissolves into emptiness and dissolution: Carel dead, Pattie working in an African refugee camp, Eugene moving into a church hostel, Muriel and Elizabeth disappearing 'into the narrow labyrinth of the city' (*TOA*, p. 227), and the Rectory itself 'a vacant shell whose significant spaces would soon be merged into the empty air' (*TOA*, p. 226).

The satanic nature of Carel's evil is developed in various ways in the next few novels; indeed, with hindsight, we are aware that its seeds were present earlier in Nick in *The Bell* and he too killed himself at the end of the novel.

The next novel, *The Nice and the Good*, begins with the suicide of Radeechy, the perpetrator of necromantic rites, but the investigation into his death exposes the evil of McGrath and gives full rein to Ducane's sensitive and rather esoteric goodness, a goodness which embraces Mary, returns Kate to Octavian and is, it seems, if we are able to believe the ending of the novel, able to bring about the redemption of McGrath. Unlike *The Time of the Angels*, this novel has what we may see as a happy ending with Ducane restoring order to chaos, with wives and husbands being reunited, with children finding their fathers again, with those yearning for love finding partners and with the charade of evil, which the investigation into Radeechy's death has uncovered, being pushed aside as of no consequence.

During the gestation of this group of novels Murdoch was concerned with the presentation of the philosophic concept of Good and with the problem of a morality of Good that can exist without belief in a

God. Some of the results of these deliberations were published in *The Sovereignty of Good* and all the novels of this period reflect to some extent the philosophical ideas which were simultaneously under Murdoch's consideration. Whilst *The Time of the Angels* is most involved with the essay 'On "God" and "Good"', however, *Bruno's Dream*, published the year before *The Sovereignty of Good,* can be seen to mirror many of the ideas to be found in the last of the essays, the title essay of the book (see note 2), in which suffering, Love and Death are matters of deep concern; the outcome of *Bruno's Dream* seems to illustrate Murdoch's thesis that Good is supreme over other concepts.

Two of the earlier novels, *An Unofficial Rose* and *The Italian Girl* had begun with a death, which acted as the catalyst for all sorts of changes in the lives of the survivors. *Bruno's Dream* begins in the consciousness of the dying Bruno but his actual death occurs only in the last sentence of the final page; it is with Bruno's attempts to come to terms with his own death and with the impact of his dying upon the living that the novel is concerned. As Bruno looks back over his life in the first chapter he, apparently unconsciously, re-arranges the apportionment of guilt for all that went wrong in it; so, he sees his childhood and adolescence blighted by a harsh and unloving father, his marriage destroyed by an uncaring wife who turns his children against him; his daughter's death by drowning is seen as terrible and without point and his surviving son, Miles, never bothers to visit him. Yet, for all the deaths and misery he revisits, the tears that stream down his face are for himself, 'Poor Bruno, poor Bruno, poor Bruno . . .' (*BD*, p. 19). His eponymous 'dream' is his pointless, frustrated life; his horror is that, just as his mother, his wife and his daughter now subsist only in his dream, he too will soon be nothing but a small part of the dream of others.

The romantic love theme bears a superficial resemblance to that in *A Severed Head*. During the course of the novel whilst Bruno lies dying, Danby, Miles, Lisa, Diana, Adelaide and Will Boase fall in and out of love and ultimately pair off, Danby with Lisa, Adelaide with Will and Miles with the muse of poetry; Diana, however, is left at the end, loving and caring for Bruno and from his suffering learning vicariously how to accept death. 'The acceptance of death', Murdoch asserts, 'is an acceptance of our own nothingness which is an automatic spur to our concern with what is not ourselves' (SOG, p. 103).

It is to this point that Bruno is finally led, through the fable of the spider and the fly enacted before him as he lies on his deathbed:

> What do they feel, thought Bruno. Had the fly suffered pain when its wings were forced back and crushed by the strong thread? Had the spider felt fear when it was in the teacup? How mysterious life was at these extremities. . . . Perhaps if God existed . . . But there was no God. I am at the centre of the great orb of my life . . . until some blind hand snaps the thread. I have lived for nearly ninety years and I know nothing. I have watched the terrible rituals of nature and I have lived inside the simple instincts of my own being and now at the end I am empty of wisdom. Where is the difference between me and these little humble creatures? (*BD*, pp. 265f.).

His dying is at first terrible for the reader because, without God and with nothing to replace God except blind fate, his whole life appears meaningless. All his musings can lead him nowhere except finally to the acceptance of his own death and an awareness of his own littleness. His death, however, releases Diana from her fears and resentments; she too finds herself able to accept the idea of death but also to see through it to the other side, which Bruno was unable to do; for her, 'love still existed and it was the only thing that existed' (*BD*, p. 272). The redeeming feature of Bruno's life is that in his death he is able to teach Diana to accept death.

The demonic aspects of the other novels of this period are less apparent here, though the twins Nigel and Will, particularly the former, seem to have some demonic qualities. Will is selfish and violent but not very intelligent; Nigel, on the other hand, like Puck or Ariel, is ubiquitous, all-knowing, all-seeing, all-hearing, a voyeur, a creature of the night who peeps into windows and passes through doors, himself unseen and unheard. He is a mischief-maker and a betrayer but his acts of betrayal are informed by a rigid sense of morality through which he betrays the two great loves of his life, his twin brother, Will, and Danby. When he discloses Will's theft of Bruno's stamp and Danby's affair with Adelaide, his actions are, perhaps, more like Christ casting the money-makers out of the temple than wanton acts of malice, for he is, simultaneously, the strongest force of good in the novel. They are acts of purification by which the sins of his loved ones are purged. To Diana, Nigel remarks:

> Maybe this is how God appears now in the world, a little unregarded crazy person whom everyone pushes aside and knocks down and steps upon. Or it can be that I am the false god, or one of the million million false gods there are. It matters very little. The false god is the true God. Up any religion a man may climb (*BD*, p. 210).

Nigel's gentle care of Bruno exceeds that of any of Bruno's family; he is for the dying man both nurse and healer and Bruno is devoted to him, covering up his occasional absences lest Danby should dismiss him. During the course of the novel Nigel saves two lives – that of Diana, when she decides to commit suicide by swallowing Bruno's sleeping tablets and that of Danby when Will is about to shoot him.

Before we first meet Nigel, he is introduced to us through the thoughts of others: for Bruno he is 'Nigel with the angel fingers' (*BD*, p. 8) who is good and gentle with the old man; Danby thinks he is 'a bit mystical' and 'rather beautiful' (*BD*, pp. 25f), whilst Adelaide sees him as a demon. As the novel proceeds we realise that he is all these things. His first appearance in Chapter 3 is accompanied by a curious stylistic change in tempo, for it is written in the Continuous Present and we view Nigel, dressed all in black, performing what appears to be a mystical religious rite, in which he attempts to achieve something like the Hindu 'at-one-ness' with God. A similar suspension of time, indicated by a change in tense, occurs on several other occasions, each such occurrence being marked by a mystical, godlike manifestation of Nigel's attributes; so, in Chapter 7 he tends Bruno with incredible gentleness, a sort of Holy Ghost 'filling the room with a soft powdery susurrus of great wings' (*BD*, p. 73) and Chapter 9, dedicated entirely to Nigel, offers him as Christ ('a sufferer in his body for the sins of the sick city', *BD*, p. 80) and finally as God ('Nigel smiles ... the tender, forgiving, infinitely sad smile of almighty God', *BD*, p. 81).

Nigel's god-like attributes are manifested in his all-embracing love. In his conversation with Diana he claims that he loves everybody;

it is love that transfigures him, transcending the fears and hates of ordinary human life but, above all, his is a selfless love. He sacrifices his love for Will, in order that Will may marry Adelaide; he sacrifices his love for Danby, taking Lisa's place in Calcutta with the Save the Children Fund, thus allowing her to return and save Danby. He is a chameleon-like mythical character, yet the reality of his spiritual love brings about changes in the lives of all those who come into contact with him.

The relationships in this novel reflect a familiar pattern in Murdoch's work, with non-identical twins, an auntie who is not an auntie, a family of men whose wives have died and two sisters who, together with the twins' cousin, are at the centre of the various love entanglements. The novel finishes, not only with all the ends tied up but with a look into the future for some of the characters and Will, the man of the theatre, who in the final tying-up of ends is credited with a knighthood, returns briefly in *The Sea, The Sea,* the knighthood granted.

In *A Fairly Honourable Defeat*, the novel which follows *Bruno's Dream,* Tallis, like Ducane in *The Nice and the Good,* finds his good pitted against Julius King's evil but, unlike Ducane, he does not finally triumph. He is himself too confused, too disorganised to be an effective saviour of others. The novel begins with Hilda and Rupert celebrating their twentieth wedding anniversary in happy mood. The sun is shining as they sit together in their London garden, gossiping about their relations and friends and acquaintances. If we are to understand the Platonic symbolism as relevant here, we must see these two who can face the sun as 'Good'. For much of the novel the weather is hot and the sun bright; even the assumptions that we may be inclined to make about Evil being associated with the dark seem to be undermined. A narrator's comment in the earlier novel, *The Nice and the Good*, itself a novel of summer heat, perhaps helps to explain the choice of weather and venue:

> There is a pointlessness of summer London more awful than anything which fogs or early afternoon twilights are able to evoke, a summer mood of yawning and glazing eyes and little nightmare-ridden sleeps in bored and desperate rooms. With this ennui, evil comes creeping through the city, the evil of indifference and

sleepiness and lack of care. At such a time the long-fought temptation is wearily yielded to, and the long-dreamt-of crime is with
shoulder-shrugging casualness committed at last (*TNTG*, p. 137).

It is in this atmosphere that *A Fairly Honourable Defeat* is played
out until it reaches its climax and the hot weather breaks, to be
followed by torrential rain.

The first words in the book are 'Julius King', spoken by Hilda.
The conversation it initiates is significant, not only because it introduces a curious minor theme of the novel – the intense desire of
most of the characters to pry into each other's lives – but also because of the comment about Julius made by Rupert and repeated by
Hilda, 'He's not a saint'. It is the 'unsaintliness' of Julius that destroys both Rupert and his marriage in an elaborate Machiavellian
plot. Murdoch herself in the discussions in Caen expounded on the
Christian symbolism in the novel: 'Tallis' she explained, 'is the
Christ figure . . . Julius . . . the Prince of Darkness, King of this
World . . . Morgan is the human soul over whom they are disput-
ing' (*Rencontres*, p. 75).

In the first five chapters the names of Julius and Tallis are on
everyone's lips; the first actual appearance in the novel of Julius,
the ex-lover of Morgan, Hilda's sister, is at a candlelit dinner to
which he has been invited by Axel and Simon. Ironically, our first
meeting with Tallis, cuckolded husband of Morgan, is on the same
evening in the same place, though he has not been invited to the
dinner. Certainly Julius gets the best of the encounter here, as he
does throughout the novel, for, unlike *Bruno's Dream*, it is a novel
in which the Evil triumph and the Good go to the wall. It may be
seen as an exploration into motiveless malignity, like the actions of
Iago in *Othello*, a demonstration that, in Julius's words: 'Evil . . . is
exciting and fascinating and alive. It is also very much more mysterious than good. Good can be seen through. Evil is opaque' (*FHD*,
p. 223).

The Shakespearean reference is, as so often in Murdoch's work,
apposite. The novel is particularly concerned with theatre, with drama
as parallel with, but distinct from, reality; the characters are constantly playing roles in parts that have been written for them by
others or by themselves. The principal playwright is Julius, playing
Shakespeare and Prospero in one: 'I was the magician', he tells

Hilda on the phone, '. . . I invented it and made it happen' (p. 415). Morgan's reciting of 'Full fathom five' (*FHD*, p. 189) preshadows the sea-change that Julius brings about in the lives of several of the characters and the death by drowning that is Rupert's part.

Many of the events in the novel, though they appear to belong to the realm of comedy, have a sinister edge. Julius's plot against Morgan and Rupert has a surface resemblance to the plot in *Much Ado About Nothing* when Don Pedro determines to bring Beatrice and Benedick 'into a mountain of affection th'one with th'other' (II.i.343f.). Julius himself calls it several times 'a midsummer enchantment' (e.g. *FHD*, pp. 263–6) and describes Morgan and Rupert as 'asses', thus bringing *A Midsummer Night's Dream* into play as well. In Shakespeare, however, the intention of the love confusions is to while away the time and to bring about a romantic conclusion; they are merry jests that end in harmony. Julius's intentions are more sinister in that, like Iago, he is seeking some sort of personal satisfaction and revenge; the attempt to attach Morgan and Rupert to each other is for their harm, not for their good, not to induce genuine love between two people free to fall in love with each other but in order to prove that he can 'divide anybody from anybody' (*FHD*, p. 234) by separating Rupert from Hilda. Though he is innocent of planning Rupert's death, he knows that if his plot works he will have destroyed a happy marriage. Just as Shakespeare creates a 'double drama' when he provides his audience with a stage audience as well as a staged action to watch in the eavesdropping scenes (see discussion above, p. 45), so Julius ensnares Simon in the eavesdropping scene at the museum and the reader observes a triple action – Morgan and Rupert, Julius's 'puppets' (*FHD*, p. 263), Simon the innocent onlooker and Julius the 'magician'. For Morgan and Rupert it is a strange moment of unreality, for Simon it is a scene of horror, involving demonic forces; for Julius it is a moment of destructive power, a power which he quickly consolidates by bending Simon to his will; for the reader it is a brief insight into the workings of evil.

The philosophy of the novel is equally destructive. Julius is so wrapped up in his own solipsistic view of himself that neither in reality nor in theory can he see any point of view but his own. Goodness he utterly rejects; as he explains to Rupert: 'It is not just that human nature absolutely precludes goodness, it is that goodness . . . is not even a coherent concept, it is unimaginable for human beings . . .' (*FHD*, p. 224). Rupert is no fit adversary in the argument for he deals in philosophic theories that can be endlessly debated. The absolutes of scientific proof leave him so bewildered that he seems not to notice that Julius has produced no real proofs at all for his argument. Even the death of God, so vehemently acclaimed by Carel in *The Time of the Angels*, is dismissed derisively. Unlike Carel, Julius does not kill himself, unlike Jake Donaghue he never finds it necessary to reassess his world. At the end of the novel, which began with his name being spoken by one who was later to become a victim of his humour, he is still entirely self-obsessed and self-indulgent. He can coolly visit a restaurant recommended by the dead Rupert; he feels that life is good, but the Platonist may notice that he does not look at the sun which 'was warm upon his back' (*FHD*, p. 447). He is the archetype of the 'Kantian man' – Lucifer.

Whilst Julius is constantly in the forefront of the action, Tallis the Christ-figure is uneasily in the background. He is the scapegoat Christ, bearing the burdens of others on his own shoulders – an erring wife, a sick and disgruntled father, a drop-out nephew. Murdoch has suggested that we find Evil more attractive than Good but in Tallis she has presented us with a believable good character through whom selfless love shines. Though he does not care enough about himself to clean his house or to prepare his food properly, he acts unerringly when resistance to wrongdoing is required; the thugs beating up the Jamaican visitor are dealt with summarily; when Julius finally confesses his plot – and it is significant that he confesses it to Tallis – he is forced to make his confession to Hilda by the sheer power of Tallis's will; and finally, Tallis banishes Julius: 'just go away . . . Go right away'. Despite this, it is Julius who triumphs and Tallis who is left defeated and weeping for the sorrows of life at the end of the novel.

As readers, our consolation can perhaps be found in the Axel–Simon subplot; the vicissitudes of love are finally resolved; Simon is able to look back happily upon the 'untouchable reality' of his past knowledge of his older brother Rupert and to look forward with joy to 'a new happiness' with Axel. Moreover, in our final view of him, he 'raise[s] his face to the dazzle of the sun', so that we know, in the mythological life of the novel, that Tallis's goodness has a successor. In the robust reality of the novel the comedy is another kind of consolation for the reader. The incident in which Julius cuts up Morgan's clothes and leaves her naked in his flat equals any of the comic scenes in earlier novels.

An Accidental Man which follows *A Fairly Honourable Defeat* rehearses many of Murdoch's major themes, though perhaps on a less intense plane than the other novels grouped together in this chapter. With regard to narration it is certainly a step in a new direction for Murdoch. Unlike all the novels that precede it, it is not divided into chapters or parts but rather is openly, often almost ramblingly narrated, with gaps on the page alone indicating a change of interest; it is a very heavily-populated novel and the multiplicity of characters freely roving through its pages are intricately intertwined. The main overt narrative device which gives shape to the novel and helps to keep the narration under control, is the use of 'letter sections' in which the plot is not so much moved forward as forced to mark time whilst we ponder on the relationships of letter-writers and recipients. The use of such a time-honoured device perhaps underlines Iris Murdoch's insistence that she is a traditional novelist, maintaining the genuine narrative skills of those who have preceded her.

These five novels show a considerable advance in Murdoch's thought. If not 'philosophic novels', they are certainly novels that embody some of the basic philosophic concepts of our time. Reading them, we cannot escape thoughts about God, about Good and Evil, about Reality and about the quality of Love. Both the characters and the movement of the plots voice arguments for us that are closely related to arguments in Murdoch's philosophic books and we are forced to see how intricately interwoven are her two major interests.

5
Metaphors for Life

The four novels to be discussed in this chapter were published at roughly yearly intervals: *The Black Prince* (1973), *The Sacred and Profane Love Machine* (1974), *A Word Child* (1975) and *Henry and Cato* (1976). Following the novels of the late 1960s with their deliberate exploration into the demonic, their third-person narration and their carefully structured form which, except for *An Accidental Man* (which we may perhaps see as a 'bridging novel'), divides them into accessible chapters, these of the early 1970s break out of the more overt formal restraints. They are generally longer, they have dispensed with the containment of chapter divisions as a formal structural device and their philosophical viewpoint is far more complex. Yet, despite the apparent formlessness of such works, there is a consuming interest in the art of novel-writing and in the general philosophy of art, *The Black Prince* particularly devoting considerable discussion to it. Though there are no chapters as such, there is an overriding formal structure, breaking the novels into parts and smaller segments and, in the case of *A Word Child*, into daily diary entries. They may also as a group be seen as some of the easiest of all Murdoch's novels for the general reader to come to terms with.

Initially, the most striking innovation in these novels is the consciously deliberate narration. The reader is made aware that a story is being told, just as an audience in the theatre must be aware that what is happening on the stage is not life but a metaphor for life. The realism is at one remove but the reader/audience is gradually drawn into the action and takes it for real. Though only three of the fourteen earlier novels are in the first person, two of the four novels now under consideration are written in the first person and in each of them there is a concentration on how the story should be told. *The Black Prince* recounts the life of a novelist whose greatest novel is *The Black Prince*. In it the enigmatic narrator tells a story which is deconstructed by more opaque forms of narration, so that the actual telling itself undermines – or, alternatively, becomes part of – the plot. The eponymous hero of *A Word Child*, Hilary Burde, lives with an obsession of order that becomes part of the novel, an obsession which makes him parcel out his personal life into separate segments, evenings dedicated to visits to specific people – his sister, his professional acquaintances, his girl-friend. He tells his own story by means of a diary of daily events in a repetitive weekly sequence which reflects not only the cyclical nature of the tale he has to tell but also the rigidity of his mind. When the cyclical order breaks down his life is disrupted and a sort of cyclical chaos arises, in which, for the second time, Hilary is responsible for the death of Gunnar Jopling's wife.

In both the third-person novels, as the titles suggest, there is, first, a duality of narration: *The Sacred and Profane Love Machine* sets the lives of two women in opposition to each other and in relation to Blaise Gavender, whose wife Harriet represents sacred love, and whose mistress Emily represents profane love. Stemming from this basic opposition, the narrative proceeds through a series of further oppositions – good and evil, truth and fantasy, life and death. The other third-person novel, *Henry and Cato*, carries this device further, interweaving stories of two lives – two school-friends whose fortunes have followed opposite paths. Whilst Cato enters the priesthood, Henry moves to the USA and settles for an academic post in a second-rate American university. It is Henry, however, who constantly displays an anxiety about morality and Cato who eventually, albeit not deliberately, commits murder. Thus we observe a diametric narrative pattern in which the overtly good moves towards evil and the apparently bad strives towards good.

Secondly, just as every so often Murdoch introduces Gothic elements into her work, so she borrows from the thriller to enhance anticipation. This thriller element was seen clearly in *The Nice and the Good* and is particularly prominent in these four novels: *The*

Black Prince begins with an apparent murder, *The Sacred and Pro-fane Love Machine* with the mysterious appearances of an unknown boy in a suburban garden, *A Word Child* with the equally mysteri-ous appearance of a coloured girl at the door of the protagonist's seedy London flat, and *Henry and Cato* with Cato's attempt to dis-pose of a revolver by surreptitiously throwing it into the Thames. It will be seen, too, that much of the violence in the novels is of the kind associated with the underworld, with women being threatened and beaten up, murders being committed, and dramatic accidental deaths.

Thirdly, God, or at least the *angst* about the loss of God, has all but disappeared, though matters of faith and the Christian God are of supreme importance in the character of Cato. The novels now contemplate right and wrong, good and evil as innately human re-sponsibilities. There is still a concern about morality, about the Good, but it is a concern that, certainly in the first three of these novels, has dropped God from its calculations. Men and women now have to face up to the consequences of their own actions, not merely without recourse to a higher authority, but often with a bland fail-ure to recognise the moral problems created when there is no higher authority to refer to.

Finally, and closely allied to the problems of morality, this group of novels is concerned with the force of love to redeem or destroy. Redemptive love takes the place of religion and, as in Plato's teaching, it purifies the emotions, moving away from the selfish and per-sonal towards the spiritual and universal. At the same time, the novels recognise love's destructive capacity which is powerfully explored; in the essay 'On "God" and "Good"' Murdoch comments that 'human love is normally too profoundly possessive and also too "mechanical" to be a place of vision' (*SOG,* p. 75) and it is this too possessive love that frequently leads to disaster in these novels.

The first of the novels of this period, *The Black Prince*, won the James Tait Black Memorial Prize in 1973 and it has been considered by many critics to be the best of Murdoch's novels. Certainly it is the most complex and intricate of them all up to this point; it is also one of the most accessible. In true thriller fashion, it begins with an imagined murder and ends with a real one. The historical Black Prince, son of Edward III, lived in the fourteenth century and

fought and died in the Hundred Years' War without ever coming
into his royal inheritance; we could, perhaps, see Bradley Pearson
as a man who fights and dies for his view of truth and love, whilst
never coming into his inheritance; it has been generally accepted,
however, that the novel takes its title from Shakespeare's *All's Well
that Ends Well* (IV.v.42), from a somewhat bawdy scene in which
the Clown declares his ability to serve 'The Black Prince, sir, alias
the prince of darkness, alias the devil'. There seems little doubt
that such a 'Black Prince' is served in this novel, but his identity is
by no means so straightforward; as Francis Marloe comments in his
'Postscript', the title of the book is 'ambiguous in I cannot readily
say how many senses' (*BP*, p. 400). If the Black Prince is the devil,
he is also Hamlet procrastinating until it is too late to act, he is
also the black Eros destructive in his love, one of the 'dark gods',
whom Honor Klein said could not be cheated. The one factor common to all these possibilities, it seems, is that none of the various
'Black Princes' achieves his potential.

Likewise, within the novel, the identity of the eponymous hero is
not altogether certain. It is Julian, dressed wholly in black, who
takes on physically the guise of Hamlet, and indeed it is her father
who is killed and lies dead at the end of the novel with 'a little
puddle of blood in his ear' (*BP*, p. 378); it is, however, Bradley –
or is it Arnold? – who is the Black Eros, for the confusion of desire within the novel suggests that both are guilty of loving too
much and too little. Arnold, like the characters in *A Severed Head*,
falls in and out of love with little or no understanding of love's
consequences. He declares love, in turn, for his wife, for Christian,
and finally, and perhaps for ever, as Peter Conradi suggests,[1] for
his own daughter, Julian; he is a romancer and a philanderer as
lightweight as his novels appear to be. Bradley, on the other hand,
comes to love late in life and falls absolutely and irrevocably, destroying in his fall his sister Priscilla, Arnold and ultimately himself. It is, too, Bradley Pearson whose initials 'B.P.' appear to point
to his identification with the Black Prince and it is, I think, worth
remembering at this point that the subtitle of his story – though not
of the novel as a whole – is *A Celebration of Love*.

Though we may weave endless patterns to account for the 'Black
Prince', Murdoch herself stated quite unequivocally in discussions
in Caen:

The 'Black Prince', of course, is Apollo . . . Loxias . . . is a name
of Apollo. Apollo is the god of art, and is also . . . a murderer . . .
who killed a fellow musician in a horrible way . . . (*Rencontres*,
p. 78).

The classical 'in-joke' is underlined in Rachel's postscript where
she accuses Mr Loxias of murder, in almost the same terms as
Murdoch's statement, dating the event as 'some considerable time
ago'. Loxias-Apollo was seen by the Greeks as a god endowed with
many different powers; not only was he god of the sun, but also he
presided over sudden death, so the summons of Bradley to the putative
death of Rachel at the beginning of the novel and to the only-too-
real death of Arnold at the end is an essential fulfilment of his
role. Indeed, if Loxias is, as he himself proposes in the 'Editor's
Foreword', Bradley's *alter ego* (*BP*, p. 9), then the suggestion that
Bradley Pearson is the Black Prince is not wide of the mark; it is
Bradley too who, throughout the novel, is bound for Patara, in classical times a city sacred to Apollo. Yet, to add to the uncertainty, it
is Rachel Baffin who takes on the Devil's part and plays out her
revenge in the novel; she is, Bradley claims, 'one of the main actors, in a crucial sense perhaps the main actor, in my drama' (*BP*,
p. 33) and the novel which begins with Arnold's fear that he has
murdered her begins too with her vows of revenge:

> I shall never forgive him. Never, never, never. Not if he were to
> kneel at my feet for twenty years. A woman does not forgive
> this ever. She won't save a man at the end. If he were drowning,
> I'd watch. . . . I won't save him at the end. I'll watch him drown.
> I'll watch him burn. . . . And I won't forgive you [Bradley] either
> for having seen me like this . . . (*BP*, pp. 40f.).

The novel proper ends with a scene which reverses the opening
incident; this time it is Rachel who wields the poker and strikes out
at Arnold; and it is Rachel who telephones Bradley begging him to
come round to her place. The descriptions, the hint of drunken violence, the vocabulary, the whole situation, closely resemble the events
of the opening scene but this time the murder is real; once more,
Bradley takes on the responsibility of trying to salvage the situation
but this time without Francis Marloe as witness; it is a fatal error.

Rachel, as Bradley recognises in his postscript, has taken a perfect revenge on the two men she had sworn never to forgive. Like Hamlet she has ceased her play-acting and in a final decisive act of genius, more than worthy of a revenge tragedy, she has triumphed, though whether she planned the whole revenge from the beginning is less than certain in a novel in which nothing is very certain. Yet she allows Bradley to be punished for her crime and her crime it undoubtedly is, for we remain unconvinced by the specious explanations given in the Postscripts written both by her and by Julian. As Deborah Johnson comments, they 'serve not only to deconstruct Bradley's account . . . they deconstruct one another'.[2]

The Black Prince is a novel encased in an outer shell of what purport to be explanations and apologies: at the beginning, the 'Editor's Foreword' from Loxias and 'Bradley Pearson's Foreword'; at the end, 'Postscripts' by Bradley, Christian, Francis, Rachel, Julian and Loxias. The story contained within this shell is told by Bradley Pearson in the first person. In his Foreword Loxias describes the story as a 'drama' and himself as a 'sort of impresario', or perhaps the 'clown or harlequin figure who parades before the curtain, then draws it solemnly back'. The Postscripts at the end are said to be by the 'Dramatis Personae'. Once more, then, we are in the position of having a play unfold before us, a play in which the actors knowingly take on roles, yet for which we the reader/audience willingly suspend our disbelief until the play is played out, the last word is spoken and we are left with 'nothing' (*BP*, p. 416).

We are presented with a play in three acts. The opening of the first part sets the scene, insisting through its vocabulary on its dramatic affinities, aware of what is 'most dramatically effective', searching for a 'deeper pattern', choosing the 'first speaker' with care, deciding how to 'frame . . . the drama'. Though both Loxias and Bradley Pearson make it clear that the story is being presented to the reader by the main protagonist, though Loxias himself has received the story from Bradley, though, until the postscripts at the end, the only point of view offered is that of Bradley, the staging of the plot encourages a willing suspension of disbelief. Bradley's setting is clearly delineated: 'a ground-floor flat in a small shabby pretty court of terrace houses in North Soho, not far from the Post Office Tower, an area of perpetual seedy brouhaha'. As so often in Murdoch, the use of London names and places acts as an anchor for the story, endowing it with a sense of reality that is gradually extended into metaphor and mock-Freudian suggestiveness; a few lines after the description quoted above, Bradley epitomises his flat as a 'cosy womb' and talks of the 'austere erection' of the Post Office Tower.

Act 1 introduces all the characters and almost all the possible love scenarios – between Bradley and his ex-wife Christian, between Bradley and Rachel, between Arnold and his wife Rachel, between Arnold and Christian, between Bradley and Francis Marloe. It prepares, too, the subplot, and hints at the possible tragic elements residing in the broken marriage of Priscilla and Roger.

The second act contains the one significant development – Bradley's acceptance of his love for Julian – and round it is built both the comic and the tragic potential of the action. When, in the third act, Bradley and Julian elope, the resolution seems to be clear but, unlike the resolutions of Shakespeare's comedies, escape from the town into the country does not serve to purge the baser elements of the story and what could have been romance or comedy descends into tragedy with the separation of the lovers, the deaths of Priscilla and Arnold and the wrongful arrest, conviction and eventual death of Bradley.

The theatrical presentation of *The Black Prince*, however, may be seen merely as a device to impose form on the wealth and multiplicity of material that Murdoch brings into the novel. One of its principal concerns is with the apprehension of life through art. Only through his narrated autobiography does Bradley's life take on meaning and reality both for himself and his readers; only by examining each event is he able finally to distinguish reality from appearance; only, even within the narrative, by reinterpreting art itself, is he able to make sense of the contingency of the events which come upon him and finally, only by the actual act of writing his memoirs is he able to realise himself as novelist and artist.

Bradley Pearson, like a number of Murdoch's protagonists, has risen from humble origins to a position, not of affluence but certainly of comfort. He and his sister Priscilla have as their childhood background their parents' unsuccessful gift-shop and newsagent's in Croydon; with both their parents now dead, Bradley and Priscilla appear to have no other blood relations, though both have made uncongenial marriages and in both instances their marriage partners have deserted them and taken on other sexual commitments.

From the outset, Bradley appears to be at pains to establish himself as indecisive and burdened with anxiety about his every move and about what attitude he should take to his acquaintances. When, however, he is faced with the first crisis – Arnold's attack upon Rachel – he acts swiftly and firmly, taking control of the situation and offering a subtly edited version of the actual events that allows Arnold to vindicate himself in his own eyes, despite his obvious guilt. It is his capacity for action, rather than his indecision, that turns out to be Bradley's tragic flaw. When he elopes with Julian and abandons Priscilla, he unwittingly provides a justification for later accusations of heartlessness on his part; when Rachel kills Arnold, Bradley's attempt to hide the truth by wiping the poker clean of Rachel's fingerprints, fuels the false case against himself.

Unlike many of the earlier novels *The Black Prince* is not really concerned with the tribulations of marriage, though we see in it the results of the failure of Priscilla's marriage and the moral oppression within that of Arnold and Rachel. Instead, the novel follows Bradley's journey of self-discovery; it is a difficult and painful experience for him. He is overwhelmed by doubts over his own identity: 'I feel the very darkness of my own personality invading my pen' (*BP*, p. 108). He is a child of confused background – an uneducated father, 'nervous, timid, upright, conventional' (*BP*, p. 82) and a mother who always felt that she had married beneath her; his desire has been to push his background behind him and recreate himself in his own image. Yet, as he himself acknowledges, he increasingly identifies himself with his father's rigidity, his father's fear of improper behaviour; this is particularly manifest in Bradley's reactions to any suggestion of sexual or marital irregularities. He is unable to accept any responsibility for his own failed marriage and claims that after the divorce he 'lived for years with a sense of things irrevocably soiled and spoiled' (*BP*, p. 25). Likewise, though he believed it impossible for his sister Priscilla to be happy with her husband, his immediate reaction when she says that she has left Roger is that she must return to him: 'You can't leave Roger. It doesn't make sense. Of course you're unhappy, all married people are unhappy' (p. 73). When Rachel proposes some sort of extramarital affair to him he is uncomfortable and stiff with her.

Is it the onset of love that finally helps Bradley to understand himself and to free himself of inhibitions? The process is nothing if not painful. Like Humbert Humbert in *Lolita*, he tries for a while to stifle his love but when he yields to it and finds that it appears to be requited, he throws all caution, all common sense, to the winds and again, like Humbert, elopes with his child-lover, for Julian is little more than a child. And where does he go with Julian? He goes to Patara, his rented cottage by the sea which bears the name of Apollo's sacred city, where he at first finds happiness. From the outset, Patara has been his goal, the place where he believed his art could develop. With Julian it becomes, albeit briefly, the summit of Bradley's achievement in love, until Apollo takes on another of his roles and the death of Priscilla is announced.

The novel is rich in classical and mythological references which serve as a framework for the action and which become enabling agents for the discussion of art and of life. In his 'Editor's Fore-word' Loxias describes Bradley's story as 'in its essence as well as in its contour a love story' and he goes on to say:

> Man's creative struggle, his search for wisdom and truth is a love story. What follows is ambiguous and sometimes tortuously told. Man's searchings and his strugglings are ambiguous and vowed to hidden ways (*BP*, p. 9).

Bradley Pearson's own 'Foreword' picks up these ideas and dis-cusses in particular the relationship between art and truth, a theme which becomes a continuing dialogue throughout the novel and which returns on several occasions to the Murdochian idea expressed origi-nally in *Under the Net*, that 'Real thoughts come out of silence' and 'Art comes out of endless restraint and silence' (*BP*, pp. 49f.). The discussion of art is a particularly significant aspect of this novel, since it appears to encapsulate many of Murdoch's thoughts about her own writing at this time.

The two novels which follow, *The Sacred and Profane Love Ma-chine* and *A Word Child* are both concerned with love – love within marriage and love outside the marriage bond – and with the moral-ity which governs love in its various manifestations. It is a theme which has been explored in several of the earlier novels, particu-larly in *A Severed Head*, although here, unlike in the earlier novel, the marriage ties are less evident. In *The Sacred and Profane Love Machine* Blaise Gavender cannot envisage giving up the 'sacred' love of his wife Harriet but he still wishes to enjoy the 'profane' love of his mistress Emily. The half-truths, the lies, the deceptions and the emotional cruelties that this involves prove finally to be insoluble, except by death. As in *A Fairly Honourable Defeat*, it is the good who suffer: Harriet dies, Luca's mind is permanently damaged, David is left in some sort of despair but Blaise and Emily survive, Emily to usurp Harriet's place as wife and take over her house.

A Word Child, published a year later, is also concerned with love outside the marriage bond and again it is shown to be utterly destructive, so that in a cyclical pattern Hilary Burde, the 'Word Child', destroys with his uncontrolled love Gunnar Jopling's first wife Anne and then, years later, Gunnar's second wife Kitty. In this novel, however, Hilary gets little joy from his illicit affairs and is made to suffer through the death of Anne and through the double pain he has inflicted on Gunnar.

Every so often in her novels Murdoch turns to oblique discussion of Christian faith and morality. It is present, though not overtly so, in *The Bell*, which is concerned with the problems of a Christian community working together; *The Red and the Green* and *The Time of the Angels* are both, at least on one level, concerned with the priesthood. *Henry and Cato* (1976), however, breaks new ground in examining Cato's conversion from atheism to Christianity, his beliefs as a Catholic priest and his ultimate anguish at his loss of faith. The problems of morality, of Good and Evil which surround him are thus seen in a religious perspective. Simultaneously, through Henry, the novel looks at problems of morality outside the Christian dispensation and again asks the question whether there can be Good without God.

The two eponymous protagonists had come together in childhood through their shared sense of oppression and their desire to establish their own identity. Their social standing and backgrounds, however, are quite different: Henry is the son, albeit the younger son, of the Marshalsons of Laxlinden Hall; Cato is the son of a scholar, a university lecturer, a failed Parliamentary candidate, a militantly atheistic father and a gentle mother who died when he and his sister

were children. The story begins when both Henry and Cato, for
different reasons, have been away from home for some years and
have more or less lost touch with each other. The opening sections
of the novel establish connections through a narrative simultaneity
which has the deliberately cumulative effect of drawing together
several threads of the tale that is about to unfold. One particular
moment in time is pinpointed for our introduction to Henry and
Cato and their families, though they are not together: Cato Forbes
is walking to and fro on Hungerford Bridge; Henry Marshalson is
in an aeroplane high over the Atlantic; Henry's mother, Gerda, and
Lucius Lamb are in the library at Laxlinden Hall, the Marshalsons'
family home; and Cato's father, John Forbes, is sitting in his kitchen
reading a letter from his daughter, Colette. We learn what has happened before this point in time only through the retrospective mental soliloquies of the various characters.

Henry's flight across the Atlantic is the result of his learning
that his older brother Sandy is dead and that he himself has inherited the ancestral home and fortune. It is not, however, the inheritance that delights him but the fact of his brother's death:

> [an] unexpected marvel had entered his life. . . . Sandy was dead . . .
> Henry flexed his toes with joy . . . Inheriting the property was
> nothing. What mattered was that bloody Sandy was no more
> (*HC*, pp. 3f.).

The section of the novel dealing with the flight is entirely presented to us through Henry's stream of consciousness; it tells us
the salient facts of his life but it also makes us aware of his wor-
ried perception about his own identity; he sums himself up in a
series of single-word concepts, all perhaps suggesting roles that he
sees himself playing: 'luxurious Henry . . . private Henry . . . Alien-
ated Henry . . . lost Henry . . . refugee Henry . . . leave-taking Henry . . .
Timid Henry . . . escaping Henry . . . tolerated Henry . . . Inferior
Henry . . . tactless Henry' and finally, as he finishes another Mar-
tini and sinks back to sleep 'drunk Henry' (*HC*, pp. 3–9).

Henry's perception of himself as a man victimised by his past,
encourages him in his determination to destroy that past, to sell
Laxlinden Hall, to settle his mother in a cottage, to get rid of Lucius
Lamb and to give his fortune away. His motives are nevertheless

confused: he feels both love and hatred for his mother and for his
old home; he professes to believe that wealth should be more evenly
distributed and that he must therefore give his money away. In the
absence of a controlling faith, however, lacking a God to guide
him, he panics, feeling like 'a man destined by dark forces to commit a murder for which he had no will and of which he had no
understanding' (*HC*, p. 59). There is a double irony in the fortunes
of the two friends for, though it is Henry who has rejected Christianity and Cato who has found it, Henry's ideas are, without his
recognising it, based upon Christian morality, whilst Cato turns from
God, tries to persuade Henry to hold on to his house and wealth
and finally becomes the one who commits a murder for which he
had neither will nor understanding.

Discussion of morality is here on a less cerebral plane than in
many of the earlier novels. In Henry we see Good without God in
action. Though he does not fulfil his initial intention on inheriting
the property – what might seem to be the Christ-directed deed to
sell all his possessions and give the money to the poor – he sets in
motion the more practical plan of building a model village on his
land. Though he does not marry the poor and lowly Stephanie, his
response of love, pity and understanding changes her life, even if
the ransom money which he leaves at her flat is left accidentally.
Above all, he responds to the demands of love: when Cato appeals
to him for help he finds that he cannot 'blindly put his friend's life
at risk' (*HC*, p. 230) so, despite his fear, he risks (as he believes)
his own life to save his friend. Finally, when the nightmare is over,
he marries Colette who loves him, and chooses happiness (see *HC*,
p. 323). It is significant that he is the first to see the kestrel, which
both he and Cato recognise as the symbol of the Holy Ghost, hovering
over the wasteland, for on his return to Laxlinden it is as though
he is guided from his selfish, self-centred life into an unexpected
goodness.

Cato, on the other hand, brought up after his mother's death by
his rationalist atheist father, sustains a blinding conversion to Christianity, like Paul on the Damascus road. Murdoch presents it in
Platonic terms: '[Cato] entered quite quietly into a sort of white
joy, as if he had not only emerged from the cave, but was looking
at the Sun ...' (*HC*, p. 26). A warning note is sounded for the
reader, however, in the words which immediately follow this quota-

tion, for Cato found the Sun 'easy to look at'. In 'The Sovereignty of Good Over Other Concepts' Murdoch had written:

> It is *difficult* to look at the sun: it is not like looking at other things. . . . The impulse to worship is deep and ambiguous and old. There are false suns, easier to gaze upon and far more comforting than the true one (*SOG*, p. 100).

Has Cato then gazed at a false sun? Certainly, he derives, at first, great comfort from his newly-embraced religion, though it alienates him from his family. For a time he lives within 'a perfect happiness' (*HC*, p. 28), exulting in the spiritual power which the confessional affords him and creating for himself the role of eccentric priest, habitually wearing a cassock and living in slum conditions among the people he purports to believe he is serving. Yet, when any personal sacrifice is required from him he fails; he is intolerant of the shortcomings of Gerald Dealman, his co-worker at the Mission; he does not bother to answer Father Milsom's letter; he is unable to give up smoking and, worse, he is unable to give up a selfish love for Beautiful Joe.

The loss of God for Cato results not only in his rejection of the priesthood, but also in the loss of truth; it is his rationalist and atheistic father whose *credo*, despite his domineering attitude towards his children, appeals to the Good in us:

> 'I believe in the good life and in trying to be a good man and in telling the truth – I think that's at the centre of it all, telling the truth, always trying to find out the truth, not tolerating any lie or any half-lie – it's the half-lies that kill the spirit' (*HC*, p. 210).

Platitudinous though this statement may seem, in it John Forbes has put his finger on his son's problem – it is Cato's half-lies that are killing his spirit: his refusal to face the fact that he is in love with Beautiful Joe and his consequent rejection of genuine love for some sort of self-indulgent but repressed infatuation; his misunderstanding of his role as carer for others and his consequent renunciation of the priesthood. Cato's return to scepticism sparks off a train of events which leaves him emotionally devastated and forces him to face up to the fact that he is not isolated man but that his actions have significance in the lives of others. Both Henry and Beautiful Joe long for his priestly approbation, though the one has no faith at all and the other, brought up a Catholic, lives without any real hope for the future and dies at the hands of Cato in an appalling mix-up which Cato alone could have averted.

During the course of the novel the moral dialectic has resulted in a complete reversal of expected roles: the 'bad' Henry has come to terms with life and is integrating himself into a family community which shows mutual love and forbearance; the 'good' Cato has cut himself off from family, friends, church and God and has committed murder. It is significant that the novel ends with an almost exact verbal recall of the opening scene, as Cato walks away from Brendan with the crucifix, instead of a revolver, in his macintosh pocket, banging irregularly against his thigh. We are not convinced, however, that it is more than an empty promise of hope, for Cato cannot return to God in his life and he seems to have no one or nothing to put in His place. In contrast to Henry's happiness, Cato is left in desolation at the novel's end.

As in many of the earlier novels, the theme of confinement and escape is prominent. Both the main characters have escaped from emotional and psychological bondage, years before the action of the novel; Colette and Stephanie make their own escapes as the novel proceeds, though Stephanie's is different in quality. It is, however, in the capture, confinement and final escape of Cato and Colette that the most theatrical incident of the novel can be seen. Its planning is more cunning than the theft of Mr Mars in *Under the Net* and its physical compulsions more absolute than the imprisonment of Hannah in *The Unicorn*. The aura of fear and sexual disgust that Beautiful Joe creates around his plot is intensified by the mixture of solicitude and threat in his attitude to Cato. His constant use of the word 'Father' when he addresses Cato reminds us of what they both have lost through Cato's betrayal of his faith. In keeping with the rather seedy nature of the whole episode, Murdoch's theatre becomes a cinema and Cato in his confinement finds his thoughts swirling around 'as if his mind were revolving and casting great coloured images onto the screen of the dark' (*HC*, p. 228). Both Cato and Colette review their lives in flashes and the readers await the outcome of the drama. It is the elegance and ingenuity of Beautiful Joe's plan itself that captures our imagination, for its full impact occurs only after the event, when we realise that we have not been viewing a gangland plot but an elaborate hoax on Joe's part. Unlike Shakespeare, Murdoch has not let her audience into the secret; we can never be sure that Colette would not have been raped and killed if Cato had not intervened.

What emerges from these four novels is a striking move forward in the investigation of evil, in which Murdoch, moving away from the demonic images of characters such as Carel Fisher and Julius King now seems to take up William Golding's stance that humankind is innately evil. Each of the four ends in deaths that have their origin in the selfishness and the self-seeking of one or more of the characters. Yet they are a sufficient proof of the contingency of life that Jake in *Under the Net* had tried to refute; even the murders in *The Black Prince* and *Henry and Cato* are brought about by a chance series of events and are by no means deliberate or calculated, whilst the deaths in the two intervening novels follow a similar accidental chain.

Henry and Cato in particular points the way to the group of novels to be discussed in the next chapter since it is vitally concerned with what we may see as the differences between religion and morality and looks specifically at Christianity as it is manifested through Cato's conversion to the Roman Catholic church. Further, it also points the way to the later novels in its increased use of a more poetic prose style, especially noticeable in the descriptions of Laxlinden Hall and its grounds.

6
The Mystic Novels

In the next six novels, from *The Sea, The Sea* (1978) to *The Message to the Planet* (1989), Murdoch appears to have moved on to a different plane of thought. These novels are deeply philosophical, deeply religious, full of mysticism and imbued with the mystery of personality to a much greater extent than earlier novels. Intrigue, treachery, death are still present but the degree of physical violence is less obtrusive; psychological domination is, however, very apparent. All the books are long, as though their author's thoughts cannot easily be contained but must spill over into greater and greater length. All, too, are concerned to some extent with God or with religion, not necessarily with the question of Good without God which vexed earlier novels but, following on from the discussion of Christianity in *Henry and Cato*, with explicit discussion of religious thought and ideas.

In *The Sea, The Sea* religious thought centres on James; though the actual discussion of his Buddhist beliefs occupies only a few pages, we are throughout made aware of his essential goodness, in contrast to Charles's apparent lack of understanding of moral concepts. *Nuns and Soldiers* (1980) recalls Cato's conversion in *Henry and Cato*; here Christianity is again put under the microscope when Anne Cavidge contemplates her (also unexpected) conversion to Catholicism and her subsequent rejection of convent life; likewise, reflection on Christian faith moves uneasily through the pages of *The Philosopher's Pupil* (1983) and occasionally breaks into more overt discussion, whilst *The Good Apprentice* (1985) looks at the possibility of a religion without God and *The Book and the Brotherhood* (1987) examines Marxism and finds it wanting. The final novel in this group, *The Message to the Planet*, suggests a search for the ultimate philosophy, the secret that lies, not behind physical life, but behind the very essence of spiritual life itself; Marcus Vallar, however, dies a mystical death with his secret, if he had one, intact. Each of these late novels carries the discussion forward a little but most noticeable is the way in which religion has, over the span of the novels, gradually come into the forefront of the moral debate which Murdoch conducts. Moreover, in these later novels the philosophical arguments about the existence of God appear to have converged upon one particular matter – the Ontological Proof of God's existence, the *a priori* proof which it seems impossible to disprove because in itself it relies on some kind of personal faith, that we cannot conceive the *idea* of God as the Supreme Being without recognising the *existence* of God because existence is greater than thought. It is this hope which, in *The Message to the Planet*, buoys up Gildas Herne at the end.

In earlier novels a repetitive theme has centred on the failed or dissident religious. Catherine Fawley in *The Bell* and Barney Drumm in *The Red and the Green*, both dedicated to a life of Christian service, the one in a convent, the other in the priesthood, never achieve their religious ambitions. *The Time of the Angels*, which follows *The Red and the Green*, offers us a renegade priest who has not only lost his faith but who appears to have sold his soul to the devil. It is not until *Henry and Cato* that a priest is portrayed who suffers such *angst* at his loss of faith that the reader is forced into direct spiritual confrontation with the question of the existence or non-existence of God, as distinct from the repeatedly philosophically argued debate on the possibility of Good without God which has permeated so many of the previous novels. This *angst* about personal faith continues in the novels under discussion in this chapter but it is continually mitigated by a determined clinging to the deep-seated conviction that a belief so ardently held must be anchored in some sort of truth.

After fifteen years in a convent, Ann Cavidge in *Nuns and Soldiers* has emerged into the world, no longer convinced of the truth of her religion but still 'soaked in Christianity and in Christ, sunk, saturated, stained indelibly all through' (*NS*, p. 67); thus, the idea of her faith creates its own existence. Father Bernard in *The Philosopher's Pupil* follows to some extent the same line of argument; like others of Murdoch's religious figures (indeed, like Murdoch herself) he is able to reject God but clings to the idea of Christ as 'a mystical figure' (*PP*, p. 156). Likewise, in *The Book and the Brotherhood* Father McAlister, having lost his own faith, struggles to save Tamar, if not her soul, at least her sanity, by inducting her into Christian belief. In *The Message to the Planet* we are presented with yet another failed priest, Gildas Herne, who has left the priesthood; yet, at the end of the novel, he is able to say to Ludens, 'I *know* that my Redeemer liveth' and express the belief that his own faith can make God live for him (*MTTP*, p. 561). As has been suggested above, *The Good Apprentice* pursues the idea of a religion without God; Stuart Cuno is obsessed with the idea of a religion based on goodness, on spirituality without God or the supernatural beliefs that accompany Christianity.

Closely allied to these religious thoughts and perhaps one of the most striking aspects of all these novels is the move towards mystic experience, even toward what at times appear to be miracles. *The Message to the Planet* contains what may be seen as a 'resurrection', a precursor of the apparent resurrection of Peter Mir in *The Green Knight*; here it takes the form of the healing of the almost dead, the clearly dying Patrick, by Marcus Vallar; the rescue of Charles by James in *The Sea, The Sea* has likewise miraculous connotations. Further, both Marcus and James appear to will their own deaths, at times and in places chosen by them. The mystic events in the other four novels may perhaps be considered as psychosomatic, occurring at moments of emotional stress, but they are often accompanied by troubling factual elements: Anne Cavidge finds Jesus in the kitchen of her flat and would believe it had been a dream except that her hand retains a burn where she tried to touch him and that the pebble he used to illustrate his parable remained on the table after he had gone; at crucial moments in their lives, both Edward Baltram in *The Good Apprentice* and Rose Curtland in *The Book and the Brotherhood* hear their names called by disembodied voices and Edward hallucinates, seeing his father Jesse on two occasions. The visions of flying saucers in *The Philosopher's Pupil* are perhaps more problematic because of the constant reports of such sightings in our own contemporary life, but that it is a mystic, if not a religious experience is made clear by George being struck blind on the equivalent of the Damascus Road, after the death of his mentor, John Robert Rozanov.

There is further experimentation with modes of narration in this group of novels. Of the two first-person novels, *The Sea, The Sea* and *The Philosopher's Pupil*, the latter uses a device which for Murdoch is new, though it has been widely used by earlier novelists, most notably by Conrad; this is the first-person raconteur, not a principal in the story but, like Conrad's Marlow, on the fringes of the action, not quite a 'god's-eye view' but a view less subjective than that of any individual actor in the drama and one which simultaneously allows the narrator to make judgements upon the characters and the action. Again, too, there is considerable emphasis on the novels as dramatic works, with careful casting and elaborate scene setting.

The Sea, The Sea is a first-person novel, much of it written, like Nigel's part in *Bruno's Dream*, in the Continuous Present, for when Charles Arrowby begins to write he knows he wants to write a book about himself but he is not sure whether it is to be a memoir or a diary, the significant difference being, of course, that a memoir will recount the past, whereas a diary will detail the day-to-day events of the present. Finally it becomes both, for in telling about the daily events of his life, the narrator recalls in retrospect, and piecemeal, his own history and intermingles the past with what is happening in his own present. The section of 'Prehistory' which introduces the story and in which Charles surveys his past life is written almost entirely in the Present Tense, whilst the long central section entitled 'History' recounts Charles's life as he is living it in the present, alternating between the immediacy of telling what is going on at the moment of telling and the sallies into the very recent past which are told in the Past Tense and serve as links in the continuity of the tale. The final 'Postscript' section again reverts to the Continuous Present. In the context of the novel the alternation of tenses is a significant narrative device, for it reinforces Charles's apparent inability to distinguish the past from the present. His retirement into what he purports to intend to be peaceful obscurity develops into a period of obsession, during which he attempts to relive a schoolboy romance with Hartley Smith, the now-ageing object of his adolescent dreamworld. The deliberate way in which the author plays with various tenses emphasises the confusion in Charles's mind between past and present and when, during Hartley's captivity, Charles asks her, 'Hartley, have you no sense of the present tense . . .?' (*The Sea*, p. 329), we realise that Charles is subconsciously blaming her for his own shortcomings; he it is who has confused the present and the past.

Furthermore, the concentration on the methods employed for narrating the novel reinforces the matter of the novel itself; in many first-person narrations we are given the impression that the narrator is simply telling a story. Here, however, as in *The Black Prince*, one of the novel's principal concerns is with the art of narration. The opening page suggests Charles's obsession with what and how he is to write, the vocabulary constantly emphasising his deliberations: 'as I write . . . I had written . . . opening paragraph . . . my memoirs . . . this chronicle . . . a page old, it feels more like a diary than a memoir' (p. 1). What Murdoch, the author, has here settled for is the immediacy of a story, the end of which is apparently not known even to the narrator. Such a method is closely akin to stage presentations and here, as in *The Black Prince*, the affinity with drama is strongly emphasised, not only in a symbolic way, as in the earlier novels but in the very stuff of the story itself. Born in the Forest of Arden and growing up close to Stratford-on-Avon, Charles Arrowby is obsessed with Shakespeare: 'Those who knew me in later years as a Shakespeare director', he writes,

> often did not realize how absolutely this god had directed me from the very first. . . . From the guileless simplicity of my parents' life, from the immobility and quietness of my home, I fled to the trickery and magic of art. I craved glitter, movement, acrobatics, noise. I became an expert on flying machines, I arranged fights, I always took . . . an almost childish, almost excessive delight in the technical trickery of the theatre (*The Sea*, p. 29).

Early in his story, when Charles is reviewing his acting and directing career, he comments that he thinks he was a good Prospero; Murdoch doubtless intends the reader to carry the analogy through. Charles, in his own story, *is* Prospero. His isolation in his house beside the sea can be equated with the ageing Prospero's isolation on his magic island at a time in his life preparatory to scores being settled and the past redeemed. Like Prospero, too, Charles embarks on the tale of his past life, though at greater length and to the reader as audience. Yet his isolation is incomplete, for, far more quickly than in Prospero's case in *The Tempest*, his past follows him in the shape of his old lovers, his theatre friends and his cousin James. Though very early in his story he claims that there 'has been a moral change' in him (*The Sea*, p. 3), even he himself is not altogether sure as to whether he has abjured his magic and drowned his book.[1] Charles's 'magic', however, is not mystical; it has been performed to win admiration, to gain praise, to ensnare women whom he has used for his own ends. It is a very materialistically based magic, the wonders of which are miraculous only to the uninitiated, and it is based, not on the intention of righting wrongs, but on 'trickery', on deceiving the eye and thereby deceiving the mind.

James, however, whom we may see as in some ways playing Ariel to Charles's Prospero, finding 'his way across country like a fox', discovering lost playthings and even 'seriously attempting to learn to fly' (*The Sea*, p. 63) in their childhood, appears to have mystic attributes: he is instrumental in returning Hartley to her husband; he miraculously saves Charles's life and finally he disappears in a liberating death which leaves Charles free to resume his own life but obsessed now with memories of James. But to see James merely as an Ariel figure belittles him. He is not just a miracle-monger, a performer of spectacular feats but rather a religious mystic, in the long line of magicians and enchanters in Murdoch's novels, running from Hugo in *Under the Net* to the later novels which are dominated by such figures.

Like Hugo, James is by no means the principal protagonist in this novel, though his influence upon Charles is profound. A trifle ingenuously, Charles comments early on in the novel that 'cousin James has never been an important or active figure in the ordinary transactions of my life. His importance lies entirely in my mind' (*The Sea*, p. 57). In his mind, however, cousin James looms large; his mystic abilities are at first merely manifested in his ability to know about what happens to Charles without being told; Charles constantly ponders 'I wonder how . . .' in relation to James (see, for instance, *The Sea*, pp. 57, 65, 173).

For the reader, James becomes the focus for the moral and religious thought in the novel. Also, at a fairly early stage, it is through

Charles's complete lack of understanding about James and perhaps also about himself that we realise the naivety and unreliability of Charles as narrator: 'I suppose [James] too has been a successful man. My own feeling that I have "won the game" comes partly from a sense that he has been disappointed by life, whereas I have not' (*The Sea*, p. 66). Charles's success, however, his apparent lack of disappointment are purely materialistic; the events which follow suggest that he is a deeply frustrated man who has achieved worldly success at the expense of his spirit. Behind the role of brash womaniser, of ruthless theatre director, it appears that there is a desolated soul, whose emotional life came to an end when his childhood sweetheart deserted him. In fact, as James attempts to make clear to him, the broken-hearted lover is simply another role that Charles assumes in order to console himself for the emptiness of his spiritual life; it is a story that he has invented to account for his life. As James explains:

> we live in dreams and by dreams, and even in a disciplined spiritual life . . . it is hard to distinguish dream from reality. In ordinary human affairs humble common sense comes to one's aid. For most people common sense *is* moral sense. . . . Ask yourself, what really happened between whom all those years ago? You've made it into a story and stories are false (*The Sea*, p. 335).

It is the very story that Charles himself is writing, a dramatic focus for a book that at first appears to have no *raison d'être*, except that of presenting the *pensées* (see *The Sea* p. 2) of a retired theatre tycoon. When he first embarks on his project and introduces himself, Charles makes no mention of his lifelong devotion to Hartley: 'I am wifeless, childless, brotherless, sisterless, I am my well-known self, made glittering and brittle by fame' (*The Sea*, p. 3). Even when he tells how he defied his mother to go to acting school and then into the theatre, there is no suggestion that he is leaving behind him the girl of his dreams (see *The Sea*, p. 30). It is only when he makes a mental survey of the women in his life that he considers Hartley and then merely as 'the girl', not by her name (*The Sea*, pp. 52f.). The unexpected appearance of an elderly Hartley *doppelgänger*, 'an old woman in the village, [with] a transient look of [Hartley's] head placed like a mask upon somebody entirely different' (p. 86), suddenly provides a focal centre for Charles's tale and simultaneously makes the use of the Continuous Present tense of such vital narrative significance. The memory of Hartley enlarges itself in Charles's mind until it takes complete possession of both his present and his past. The kidnapping and incarceration of Hartley which follows is reminiscent of Beautiful Joe's capture and imprisonment of Cato Forbes and is yet a further example of Murdoch's use of the theme of freedom and captivity, for in each case it is the kidnapper who is in moral and spiritual captivity.

Yet, despite the apparent insubstantiality of Charles's memories of Hartley, the novel is about love and about love seen in the perspective of good and evil. The Hartley of his imagination represents the only purely unselfish love he has known, a spiritual love without carnal possession; through his memory of this love, Charles is striving to return to innocence, to wipe out the evil and corruption that has intervened and to become morally 'Good' again. However much it is also mere fantasy, his love for Hartley has in it a redemptive power until Charles debases it by attempting singlehandedly to do as Gilbert says that he and Lizzie have done together, 'we've sort of repossessed the past together and redeemed it' (*The Sea*, p. 93). The past cannot be 'repossessed'; one has to live in the present with the past focused in it and Charles has to learn to live with his past; before he is able to do so he must endure afresh the anguish of lost love, not only in the loss of Hartley but also and more poignantly in the loss of Titus and finally of James. There is a sense in which the loss of innocence pervades all these later novels, accompanied by the Miltonic understanding that innocence is not goodness. Charles appears unable to accept that he cannot return to a state of innocence.

Interwoven with Charles's story is a second tale which he appears to tell almost unaware, of the mystic tie that unites two people, of the way in which his own search for identity discovers his cousin James to him and of James's mystic Christ-like qualities. James creeps quietly into the story on page 4 when Charles remembers a comment he had once made about 'people who end their lives in caves'. Charles appears to have misunderstood this remark and believes that Shruff End is his cave and is a good place to end his life; but we can have no doubt that Murdoch's reference is once more to Plato's cave, from which the Good must emerge to look at the sun. It is a hint that James is striving towards Platonic goodness and that while he understands that many people never escape the cave, he himself aspires to emerge from the dark and look at the sun. As the novel proceeds its focus switches to James, even though the surface story is still concerned with Charles. Yet James has been present from the very beginning: in telling of his own childhood, Charles simultaneously talks about his cousin, whom he, by turns, has envied and admired and pretended to despise throughout his life.

The deliberately offhand way in which Charles constantly refers to James makes us realise not only the extent to which he is really obsessed by James's life but also his self-absorption which leads to his lack of understanding of the spiritual and mystic qualities of his cousin. Charles, like many characters in earlier novels, is entirely engrossed with himself and it is not until almost the end of the novel that his solipsism is jolted and he is forced to reassess the story he is narrating.

James appears in person about a third of the way through the book to perform his first rescue of Charles who has a fainting fit whilst visiting the Wallace Collection during a brief return to London from his seaside sanctuary. As always, Charles is bewildered by his cousin's opportune presence:

> I wondered how long James had been watching me in the picture gallery before I noticed him, and why indeed he had been there at all on that particular day at that particular hour (*The Sea*, p. 173).

James's next appearance is at Shruff End, about two-thirds of the way through the book. In fact, Charles's retirement to Shruff End and his attempted self-isolation is of brief duration, almost non-existent, for his solitude is constantly invaded by acquaintances from the past – Gilbert, Lizzie and Rosina are frequent visitors and for a while Gilbert becomes butler-cum-housekeeper for Charles; James arrives at what in a Shakespearean comedy would be a significant moment, when most of the cast of the plot seem to be gathering together at Shruff End and when Hartley emerges for the first time from the bedroom that is her prison cell to be viewed by the whole of the assembled company as she begins to descend the stairs. It is a moment of dramatic spectacle such as we have seen staged in *The*

Bell or *The Unicorn* and shall see again in later novels.

With James's arrival, the whole atmosphere changes; not only does Hartley decide to take the initiative and demand her release but James becomes 'a centre of magnetic attraction' (*The Sea*, p. 328) and the main focus of a plan to help Charles and to free Hartley. It is the beginning of a violently dramatic period of a few days during which Hartley is returned to her husband, Charles is pushed into Minn's Cauldron and rescued by James and Titus is drowned. In each of these events James's role is significant: he masterminds the plan to return Hartley; he performs the impossible, the miraculous rescue of Charles and he feels in some way diminished because he fails to save Titus just as he had failed to save the Sherpa in their night on the Tibetan mountain pass.

The moral weight of *The Sea, The Sea* rests on James; he, like Tallis in *A Fairly Honourable Defeat*, is the saint, though, unlike Tallis, he does not have to battle against a truly demonic figure and his powers of goodness appear to embrace magic. On his last visit to Charles at Shruff End he seems to pave the way for his own death, not only by clearing up all earthly misunderstandings, but also by hinting at the 'journey' he is about to take. It is on this final visit that the most serious discussion in the novel on the question of goodness and of religion takes place: 'Goodness', he tells Charles, 'is giving up power and acting upon the world negatively' (*The Sea*, p. 445). It is perhaps a message for Charles, who despite his apparent withdrawal from the world, has attempted to hold on to his power over his friends and over events; simultaneously, however, it is a statement of James's own intentions: 'The last achievement is the absolute surrender of magic itself, the end of what you call superstition' (*The Sea*, p. 445). He is himself undergoing the process of surrendering everything.

His subsequent death – or disappearance – is his final mystic act. Neither Charles nor the reader is entirely certain that he is dead: Charles toys with the idea that his 'death' has been manipulated by the Secret Service and that James is on a very secret mission to Tibet; the reader has the uncomfortable and perhaps somewhat irrational feeling that he has been 'translated' to another sphere, like Harry in Eliot's *The Family Reunion*. Certainly the account of his death given by Dr Tsang is itself enigmatic; he seems to see James as having attained the Buddhist state of Nirvana, as having freed himself from the Wheel (see *The Sea*, p. 385). Tsang claims that he is an Indian but he comes from Dehra Dun in the north of India, close to the Tibetan border; his name suggests that he is of Tibetan origin and we might well assume that he himself is a Buddhist, so a Buddhist interpretation of James's death is not surprising.

The immediate effect of James's death on Charles is a beneficent one. The fearful sea-monster, which Charles believes is evil incarnate and which manifests itself to him at the beginning of his story and again during his ordeal in Minn's Cauldron is replaced by the 'wet doggy faces' of four seals (*The Sea*, p. 476) which he believes have come to bless him. Moreover, his thoughts of James make him realise that he had loved his cousin and it is soon clear that he misses James more than he misses Hartley whom he had thought of as his first love: 'Who is one's first love? Who indeed', he asks himself (*The Sea*, p. 476).

As the novel draws to its end it is clear that Charles has reached a new understanding of himself as he writes:

> this chattering diary is a facade, the literary equivalent of the everyday smiling face which hides the inward ravages of jealousy, remorse, fear and the consciousness of irretrievable moral failure (*The Sea*, p. 483).

It is a recognition of himself as an unreliable narrator and the beginning, perhaps, of self-understanding. Whether he achieves salvation is doubtful, however. At the end we leave him back in the world that he had earlier deserted for the solitude of Shruff End, visiting the theatre, considering taking up his old job as a theatre director again, thinking of responding to a tempting invitation from Japan and arranging to go out to lunch with Angela Godwin, Peregrine's stepdaughter.

Like many of the earlier novels, *The Sea, The Sea* has once more put love under the microscope. Most of Charles's affairs may be seen as lustful escapades as well as the exercise of power but in the Hartley episode he constantly measures all the others against the pure, the innocent love he once feet for Hartley. Furthermore, Murdoch again examines the compulsions of marriage; Ben and Hartley hardly appear to have a happy marriage but they feel bound to each other and the marriage between Peregrine and Rosina which Charles destroys is restored when Rosina realises that Peregrine was willing to kill Charles for her sake.

The usual Murdochian family convolutions are absent from *The Sea, The Sea*, as they are too from *Nuns and Soldiers* (1980) which follows; though we find an extended family in the latter novel the relationships do not impinge upon the problems of the main protagonist, except in that it is clear that the family oppose Gertrude's second marriage. *Nuns and Soldiers* begins, not with a death, but with a dying. Unlike *Bruno's Dream*, however, it is the aftermath of death, rather than the dying which is at the centre of the novel. The pattern of loving and not loving, of love untold, of love felt but not offered is on a much deeper plane than the farcical accounts of love exchanges in many of the earlier novels. It is less comic and more sombre than the novels which precede it.

In the next novel, *The Philosopher's Pupil*, most of the usual love infidelities and complications are in the past when the plot opens; their results, however, are evident in what the narrator calls the *dramatis personae* set before us: Tom and his half-brothers, George (the eponymous protagonist) and Brian, and John Robert Rozanov, the philosopher, and his granddaughter, Hattie. The novel itself is less concerned with love than with obsessive relationships; George's devotion to his old teacher Rozanov is equalled by the incestuous passion of Rozanov himself for Hattie. Obsession is likewise very much to the fore in the next novel.

The Good Apprentice (1985) once more concerns itself with intricate relationships, for Edward Baltram has more than his fair share of relations and half-relations, with two mothers, two fathers, a half-brother who is not a brother at all, a half-sister and another half-sister who is probably not a sister at all. Furthermore, Edward's stepfather, Harry Cuno, is in the middle of an affair with Midge, his dead wife's sister and Edward's aunt on his mother's side. It is, however, on Edward's desire to reclaim his true father and consequently to find himself that the novel is focused.

The very title of the novel is ambiguous, for we come to realise that Edward Baltram, the eponymous hero, is not a *good* apprentice but is rather undergoing an apprenticeship to *become* good. The opening of the novel indicates the initial lack of goodness in Edward, for it begins by equating him with the biblical Prodigal Son and it proceeds to describe how he has 'sinned against heaven and before [his father]' (*GA*, p. 1) by duping his best friend, Mark Wilsden, into eating a drugged sandwich and then leaving him alone; whilst Mark experiences a euphoric 'trip' in which he falls out of the window of Edward's second-floor flat, Edward is being seduced by Sarah Plowmain, a fellow-student. At the same time we may see Edward's desperate feelings of guilt as a sign that he is essentially 'good', unlike Julius King in *A Fairly Honourable Defeat*, whose demonic qualities left him unrepentant at being the cause of Rupert's death. The rest of the novel charts Edward's journey towards repentance, atonement, redemption and the completion of his apprenticeship.

The graphic evocation of Edward's depression following Mark's death is the beginning of the dialogue about Good and Evil in the novel. He feels the burden of sin upon him. 'How does one live', he ponders, 'after total wickedness, total failure, total disgrace?. . . Like Cain I have killed my brother whom I loved' (*GA*, pp. 10 and 12). Edward's depressive illness is partly replicated in his half-brother, Stuart Cuno, who has renounced the world of science and mathematics in which he excelled, and is suffering, according to his relations and friends, from 'a temporary fit of religious mania' (*GA*, p. 34). He has abandoned his academic studies, bound himself to celibacy and is seeking a way of life that will not conflict with his new-found principles; for Stuart, the answer to the world's problems is 'goodness . . . some sort of spiritual ideal and discipline . . . religion without God' (*GA*, p. 31). So the two brothers, the one with a burden of guilt, the other with a burden of unfulfilled longing, are both seeking for some spiritual solution to their problems.

Part of Edward's trouble is that he rejects the possibility of consolation and thus of forgiveness: 'There's no morality', he asserts (*GA*, p. 45) and this belief leaves him without hope, for if there is no morality he did nothing wrong and his guilt has no point; thus there is no way in which expiation can be achieved, for there is nothing to expiate. It is this terrible sense of emptiness, of nothingness, that he has to overcome in his apprenticeship to Good. Despite their renunciation of God, there is a curiously religious tone to the struggles of the two brothers. In his attempt to help Edward, Stuart recommends him to try praying, if it is only to ask to be

delivered from evil; he commends Christ to him, he offers him a
Bible. Edward, for his part, after initially throwing the Bible across
the room, momentarily distracts himself by opening it at random, to
see if it can offer him a message, which indeed it does, for his
finger lights on a verse from Ezekiel 7.25, 'Destruction cometh,
and they shall seek peace and there shall be none . . .'. It is peace,
which Edward has been seeking but seems unable to find and which
in the *sors* appears to be withheld from him.

The desperate grasping at superstition which leads Edward to take
a *sors* from the Bible, leads him next to Mrs Quaid's seance where,
again, he appears to receive a sign, inviting him to return home to
his father and he becomes convinced that he, the Prodigal Son, must
find his real father, Jesse Baltram. Part of the mysticism of the
book arises from the apparent belief in 'signs'; a kind of religious
superstition has replaced religion itself; Edward is led through a
series of mystic 'signs' to claim Jesse as his father. As the novel
progresses he has to take lessons in Goodness and he is conducted
on his way by various teachers. His first helper is his half-brother
Stuart who, like Tallis in *A Fairly Honourable Defeat*, is a kind of
saint. He is at the centre of most of the discussions about religion
and about Good that are to be found in the novel and all his thoughts
are directed towards leading a life of purity, to subduing self and
all selfish desires and dedicating himself to the service of others.

In earlier novels there has been continual dialogue about the possibility of Good without God, of morality based on a code of values that does not have religion at its centre; in Stuart we observe a
man who is striving to establish some such precepts but faced with
Edward's desolation his most efficacious advice is to read the Bible
and to pray. Edward's uncle, Thomas McCaskerville, one of Murdoch's
'magicians' also acts as a guide; he is a practising psychiatrist and,
although Murdoch generally treats psychiatrists rather cynically,
Thomas is seen as an intuitive healer who is able to help the spir-
itually damaged, such as Edward, because he cares for them. Thus,
he reinforces the message of the seance and sends Edward to Seegard
to seek out Jesse and later persuades him to return to the flat where
he committed his crime in order to help him to placate the spirit of
guilt.

At Seegard the process of healing begins, for Edward, despite his
self-absorption, is gradually drawn into the life there and finds love

again, not sexual love but the chaste love of a brother for his sisters. The household at Seegard is one of Murdoch's more eccentric ones, following a mode of life inspired by some sort of William Morris socialism; each member of the household has her appointed tasks and they live a simple life of self-sufficiency, growing their own food, baking their own bread, making their own wine, even making their own furniture and weaving their own clothes. It is a life of disciplined order as Ilona explains to Edward: ' "Times of silence . . . times for rest, times for reading, it's like a monastery" ' (*GA*, p. 108). The simile of the monastery is apposite, for the descriptions of life at Seegard recall the William Morris type of life at Imber Court in *The Bell*. Both are artificial, somewhat whimsical but both serve to heal troubled minds, at least for a time. The ordered life suits Edward; it gives him occupation and helps him to forget, if only briefly, his black misery.

If the healing process is to continue, however, Edward knows that he must follow the signs and find his father, yet Jesse is absent; it was, he felt, his father's summons that brought him to Seegard and he is unable to rest until there is a successful outcome to his quest: 'he needed Jesse: Jesse's wisdom, Jesse's authority, Jesse's love. Nothing else would do' (*GA*, p. 152). Like the biblical Prodigal Son, he has descended to the depths of degradation; now he seeks to return to his father and ask forgiveness for the past, an act which alone can heal his wounds. The rediscovery of curiosity indicates that Edward's cure is being slowly accomplished and, on the afternoon when he finds himself alone at Seegard, it is curiosity that leads him at last to his father and to confirmation of his own identity. But the discovery of his father is not entirely beneficial, for Edward begins to see himself as at the centre of some magic rite which has absolved him from his sin in relation to Mark but has placed him in bondage to his father:

> I thought I was mad because I was in love with Mark and couldn't go on living. Wasn't that why I came [to Seegard]? To lose the old hated self and be given a new one by magic. I was in love with Mark – and now I'm in love wiht Jesse. Is that my cure, my healing, my longed for absolution? One thing I can be sure of: there are awful penalties for crimes against the gods (*GA*, p. 202).

His obsessive love for Jesse, however, is only a stage along the
way in his apprenticeship; it is still self-interest that dominates him
and he has to learn to consider and care for others.

As in *The Sea, The Sea*, the action reaches a climax when most
of the principal characters gather together at Seegard, as if drawn
by some magic. It was Thomas who, through the agency of Mother
May, had engineered Edward's first visit to Seegard, but the arrival
of Stuart appears to have been entirely orchestrated by Mother May;
in the realm of the spirit, however, the reason for it remains obscure until the arrival of Harry and Midge, drawn to Seegard it
would seem by some mystical force beyond their control in order
to prepare for the *dénouement* about to take place. In the scene
which follows, Jesse reincarnates his love for Chloe, Edward's mother,
through embracing her sister Midge; he turns an accusing finger
towards Stuart, who has allowed himself to become a 'dead' man
through withdrawing himself from the world and he takes his last
farewell of his son Edward. At the same time, Midge and Harry's
affair is brought out into the open and Edward's love for his father
is declared in front of Mother May.

Everyone's world is turned upside down by this incident: Jesse
disappears; Edward, after an inconclusive visit to Brownie Wilsden,
Mark's sister, and after hallucinating about a dead Jesse in the river,
goes to search for his father in London; Ilona leaves Seegard and
flees to London where she becomes a stripper in a night club;
Midge finds herself no longer in love with Harry and Stuart begins
to consider his future in realistic terms. Though he does not realise
it at the time, it also leads to Edward's return to life, as he shifts
from a self-centred to an other-centred existence. He first begins a
long, desperate and frenzied search for his father, tracing Jesse's
earlier life in London, visiting his old haunts and meeting his one-
time homosexual lover, Max Point, but from all this evolves a feeling
of love and care for many of those he meets, though he does not
always follow his own inclinations towards Good: he desires to
protect Ilona as sister, he wants to do something to help Max Point,
he spends time helping Midge, he telephones Meredith and, when
he returns to Seegard and finds Jesse's will which leaves everything to Edward himself, he decides that the women need the money
more than he does and destroys the will.

By the end of the novel Edward's apprenticeship is complete: he has not forgotten the past but he has come to terms with it and assimilated it into his present being: he has realised that he will get better, though his misery might not entirely disappear. Furthermore, Good is entering his life:

> A picture of ordinary happiness came to him suddenly as a blue sea and a jostle of boats with huge coloured stripy sails. He thought . . . I'll try to do some good in the world, if it's not too difficult, nothing stops anyone from doing that (*GA*, p. 517).

Stuart, too, is cured and has decided on his future as a teacher. Midge and Thomas are back together again; Meredith is frisking with his puppy; even Harry is moving towards a new life, with the possibility of a new affair with his publisher in Italy.

The Good Apprentice is built around two 'enchanter' figures, Thomas McCaskerville and Jesse Baltram. Thomas's active part in the plot is the greater; he is a saintly character who constantly tries to help others but, being too trusting, he lacks the ability to help himself. Jesse, on the other hand, is the wasted magician, whose powers are waning; like James in *The Sea, The Sea*, however, he brings about final reconciliations before his death which perhaps, again like James, he has arranged and willed.

An enchanter figure is at the centre of each of the two novels which follow, *The Book and the Brotherhood* and *The Message to the Planet*. Neither David Crimond of the former, nor Marcus Vallar of the latter are very likeable characters as far as the reader is concerned but both act as magnets to most of the other people in the two novels. Both appear to be actively searching for some solution to mankind's problems – or is it that men and women so much believe in the possibility of the alleviation of the human condition that they create their own gods? *The Book and the Brotherhood* seems to me a less successful novel than *The Good Apprentice*, partly because the centre of magnetism, the enchanter David Crimond, is unsympathetic but also because he never becomes fully integrated into the world of the novel itself. His intellectual hold on the minds of his Oxford friends who, at first against the odds, persist in believing in and supporting the writing of his *magnum opus*, the great seminal neo-Marxist book, is not quite credible; this is particularly so in view of the violence and malice of his behaviour towards Duncan Cambus and of his total lack of interest in any of them except Jean Cambus. The major problem is, I think, that the reader does not really believe in the 'book' and is not convinced by Gerard's praise of it when it finally appears. *The Message to the Planet* centres on the philosopher Marcus Vallar who is searching for a formula which will explain life, but if he finds it before his death, he takes it with him to his grave.

The six novels in this group are not essentially about God but they are concerned with morality, with religion, with the concept of Goodness, with truth and with characters who have mystical powers which affect most of the other people with whom they come into contact. Symbolically the novels examine the ontological proof of God's existence by suggesting that the belief in the essence of the magician creates the magician himself.

7
The Green Knight

Between the publication of *The Message to the Planet* and *The Green Knight* (1993) Murdoch published the most extensive of all her philosophical works, *Metaphysics as a Guide to Morals* (1992). For the reader of her novels it is not compulsory reading but it is a fascinating expansion of, and reflection on, many of the themes she has dealt with in fiction, particularly in the later books. We can see, too, how the novels themselves reflect her philosophical ideas:

> We fear plurality, diffusion, senseless accident, chaos, we want to transform what we cannot dominate or understand into something reassuring and familiar, into ordinary being, into history, art, religion, science (*MGM* pp. 1f.)

or, we might add, into novels which are able to reinstate the old mythologies whilst simultaneously exploring the contemporary problems of morality which we have been faced with ever since Nietzsche declared the death of God.

The struggle in the novels to set out some sort of 'guide to Goodness', which has become more acute as time has progressed, is here argued more singlemindedly; the adversaries in Murdoch's search for truth are not here, as in the novels, wayward characters tossed about by the contingency of being, in a world where order is constantly at odds with chance, but fellow-philosophers who have pursued or are pursuing their own solutions to the problem of morality. What is especially valuable to the reader of her novels is that certain philosophical concepts, as Murdoch understands them and as she employs them in her fiction, are discussed minutely and are considered from various points of view. Of particular interest to the reader of her novels is the dialectic concerning the connections between language and truth which runs throughout the book. At the end of such discussions we are left in no doubt as to Murdoch's own philosophic stance, though she is never dogmatic. She reaffirms her admiration for Platonic philosophy; she questions the validity of the structuralist argument; she offers a detailed investigation of Derrida's ideas and – even if ever so kindly – finally dismisses them with a cogent examination of value:

> The fundamental value which is lost, obscured, made not to be, by structuralist theory, is truth, language as truthful, where 'truthful' means faithful to, engaging intelligently and responsibly with, a reality which is beyond us. . . . 'Truth' is learnt, found, in specialised areas of art where the writer (for instance) struggles to make his deep intuitions of the world into artful truthful judgment. This is the truth, terrible, delightful, funny, whose strong lively presence we recognise in great writers and whose absence we feel in the weak, empty, self-regarding fantasy of bad writers (*MGM*, pp. 214f.).

Metaphysics as a Guide to Morals is by far the longest of her philosophical books, which, unlike her novels, have been, until this point, short and concerned with certain limited aspects of philosophical thought. Like her first published book, *Sartre: Romantic Rationalist*, however, it is intricately bound up with the discussion of the way that language works and can be usefully seen as an aid to the understanding of what she as novelist expects to achieve in her novels: it examines the question of Good without God which has been a matter of concern in so many of the novels as well as in the earlier philosophical work; it considers the place of religion in the modern world; it looks at the concepts of good and evil, of truth, of duty, to pick out just a few of the themes relevant to the novels; and it devotes a chapter to the ontological proof of God's existence, which we observed in Chapter 6 above has become increasingly a topic in the more recent novels. It almost inevitably seems to lead us to the novel which follows it, *The Green Knight*.

This latest novel melds together aspects of the Christian myth with those of Arthurian legend. It is a heavily symbolic novel which tantalises and exercises the mind with snatches of quotations, will-o'-the-wisp recalls, and well-known references, the relevance of which is often simultaneously obvious and more subtly obscure, offering the reader an immediate link with observed reality, yet leaving the imagination space in which to expand.

The novel begins in Kensington Gardens on a chilly, wet October day, when two middle-aged women, old friends since their schooldays, are walking, exercising Bellamy's dog, Anax, himself one of the principal characters in the book. Through the conversation of Louise Anderson and Joan Blacket we are introduced to most of the other characters as well as to what at first appears to be the focal centre of the plot – the death of an assumed mugger at the hands of Lucas Graffe, a scholarly academic historian, friend of both the Anderson and Blacket families and, as Joan says, an 'eccentric'. The first words of the novel, however, should alert us to the current of 'fairy' or magic which is to underlie the plot: '"Once upon a time there were . . ."'. They are the words that begin a thousand fairy stories and, with intentions at least partially similar to Murdoch's, Joyce's *A Portrait of the Artist as a Young Man* begins with the same words, as Stephen Daedalus's father tells him a bedtime story.

Joan and Louise are immediately placed at opposite poles in the black and white of fairy story, Joan the 'bad girl', Louise the 'good girl', Joan's life one of 'lawlessness' and 'disorder', Louise 'docile' and bringing into their joint lives the 'soothing possibility of order' (*GK*, p. 1). Joan and Louise are by no means at the moral centre of the story but to some extent the two women are reflected in the Graffe brothers who are, for despite the reputation of reserve he has fostered in the minds of his acquaintances, Lucas resembles no one so much as Julius King in *A Fairly Honourable Defeat*, whilst his younger brother Clement is the anxious worrier about moral rectitude whose desire for truthfulness is constantly put at risk by Lucas.

The fairy-tale element of the novel is reinforced through Louise's three daughters, but especially through Moy, the youngest of the 'three little girls' in Joan Blacket's fairy story. For Moy, everything around her is imbued with life, can think and can feel, and she experiences somewhat whimsical mystic happenings when the stones which she has collected with such loving care move about in her room; apparently even Anax observes this phenomenon. A rather heavier symbolism rests on Moy, however, when her anthropomorphism leads to her encounter with the swan in the Thames, an incident recalling the classical story of Leda and Zeus and suggesting her as the chosen of the gods; later, at the end of the novel, the 'silkies' call her back to join them in the sea but the sea-myth is thwarted by Anax, who helps his master, the spiritually-inclined Bellamy to save her.

The Green Knight has many of the attributes of a thriller, though it is certainly not a 'whodunnit' for we know from the outset who commits the murder. What we do not know is the identity of the victim or even for sure whether he was indeed murdered, for, like the legendary Green Knight, he appears to rise phoenix-like from his own ashes. When Louise first observes Peter Mir, despite the darkness, she notices his green umbrella. We soon become aware that green is Peter's colour; he wears a 'dark green tweed jacket' (*GK*, p. 103), a 'chic green tie' (*GK*, p. 122), a 'sort of green' suit (*GK*, p. 194) and he claims to be a member of the Green Party (*GK*, p. 194). It is Aleph who first suggests that he is the Green Knight. Certainly, like the Green Knight, he was struck down by a blow to the head and he undergoes resurrection (thought not immediate resurrection) to challenge Lucas on moral grounds. There are many similarities with the story of *Sir Gawain and the Green Knight* but there are also many differences, and after Peter's second death Clement ponders on the original mediaeval story and concludes that 'it's all mixed up' (*GK*, p. 432); but by this time Clement has seen clearly 'what is fundamental . . . Peter saved my life and gave his life for me' (*GK*, p. 430); the evangelical Christian ring to these words makes us realise that if Peter Mir is the Green Knight from pagan romance, he is also a Christ-figure.

Like Christ, he is a Jew and his physical characteristics are Jewish; like Christ, he is unmarried; more significantly, however, it is constantly emphasised that he died to save Clement: even Lucas acknowledges that 'one man can die for another' (*GK*, p. 91). He suffers physical pain before his death; he is resurrected and he seems to offer the possibility of redemption. It would not be merely simplistic but wrong to suggest that Peter, when he regains his memory after reliving his death experience, changes from the pagan Green Knight to the Christian hero, for the Green Knight himself was chivalrously moral, offering a challenge and a test to the knights of King Arthur's court; furthermore, Peter claims to have recovered his understanding of the Buddhist, not of the Christian, faith for, like James in *The Sea, The Sea,* he had become a Buddhist, though the blow on his head had made him forget this. We may perhaps see, however, this second experience as akin to the Pentecostal fire, which brings about a change from the Old Testamant Dispensation of justice – an eye for an eye – to the New Testamant Dispensation of mercy and love. The two myths continue to run parallel to each other; Peter offers the Green Knight's token punishment to Lucas but his [Peter's] second death is that of Christ; as a representative of Christ, Peter has died, first to save Clement and secondly to break all spells and set everyone free (see *GK*, p. 448). At his 'Last Supper' – the party at his house – which follows his resurrection into the fulness of life and precedes his second death, twelve invited guests arrive and he talks to each of them in turn; when Tessa arrives, she is both the thirteenth – the bringer of ill-luck – and the betraying Judas. Once more it is all mixed up! What is not mixed up, however, is the fact that the novel is again struggling with the problems of morality, of Good and Evil, of the place of God and religion in a godless world.

The moral theme is explored in various ways. Bellamy James is the main seeker after God, his whole life 'a religious quest' (*GK*, p. 23), which his conversion to Roman Catholicism has not resolved. Like Cato in *Henry and Cato* he considers entering the priesthood but does not do so; rather, like Catherine Fawley in *The Bell* he decides to give up the world and enter a monastery in an enclosed order, to cut himself off from social life and dedicate himself to Truth. Much of the serious religious discussion in the novel is to be found in the exchange of letters between Bellamy and his mentor, Father Damien, whose philosophy seems in many ways to accord with that of Murdoch herself.

Even without Father Damien to tell us, however, we are aware that Bellamy has romanticised the religious life, that the monastery is to be for him an escape from reality and that, moreover, he is playing a Christian role to disguise from himself the very fact that he has not convinced himself of Christ's existence, first in the flesh and then in the spirit: 'if we have a mystical Christ can that be the real Christ? Is a mystical Christ "good enough"? Could there be

Christ if *that* man never existed at all?' (*GK*, p. 41). Here he is rehearsing one of Murdoch's own worries:

> Perhaps (I believe) Christianity can continue without a personal God or a risen Christ, without beliefs in supernatural places and happenings, such as heaven and life after death, but retaining the mystical figure of Christ occupying a place analogous to that of Buddha: a Christ who can console and save, but who is to be found as a living force within each human soul and not in some supernatural elsewhere (*MGM*, p. 419).

This is the very position that Bellamy adopts after Father Damien tells him that he has lost his faith and just before what he, Bellamy, is to interpret as the vision on the road to Damascus when he sees Peter burning in the Pentecostal fire. It is not an orthodox Christian belief but is based on the dictum of the thirteenth-century Christian mystic, Meister Eckhart, which Father Damien refers to in several of his letters to Bellamy: 'do not seek for God outside your own soul' (*GK*, p. 266). Bellamy returns to this concept later in his conversation about religion with Peter Mir and it is one that is discussed minutely again and again in *Metaphysics as a Guide to Morals*; it is able to fit in with the modern rejection of God but at the same time to retain a faith in a 'Good-based' morality; it is this contemporaneity of thought which makes Murdoch revere Eckhart as 'a thinker for today' (*MGM*, p. 354).

Though Bellamy has lost his vision of a personal God he has not lost his desire to have an 'avatar' or a 'mediator' whom he can venerate; he is a man for whom religion is a necessity and he believes that he has received a sign; Peter is to be his path to goodness, yet, when Peter is taken away to Dr Fonsett's clinic, it is Emil who solves the realistic problems of Bellamy's life: 'You will stay with me . . . You must get your dog back' (*GK*, pp. 372f). We have been strangely affected by the plight of Anax for, despite the love bestowed on him by Moy, his loyalty to the master who has deserted him is absolute; early in the novel, through Moy's anthropomorphic interpretation of Anax's mind, the dog too enters the realm of religious thought in almost the very words spoken by Mary Magdalene when she found Jesus's empty sepulchre (see *GK*, p. 21 and St John, 20, 2 and 13). His reconciliation with his master when he is reclaimed helps Bellamy to find his purpose in life:

> 'I've got so much to do, I'll find that job [Father Damien] spoke of, and yes he was right about happiness, don't be miserable thinking you can't be perfect...' (*GK*, p. 471).

Quite a different sort of goodness is apparent in Moy. A vegetarian by conviction because of her concern for all living things, she is the youngest of the three Anderson girls and she celebrates her sixteenth birthday during the course of the novel. She is seen as a strange child, even by her friends and relations, for she appears to live in a slightly different world from them, a world in which everything, animate and inanimate, is endowed with its own life. Under such circumstances ordinary life becomes almost untenable and she is in a constant agony of apprehension about the feelings of such natural objects as rocks and stones. Her 'goodness', however, is Milton's 'fugitive and cloistered virtue', a kind of naïve innocence which has not had to cope with temptation:

> Aleph said, 'Innocence can't go on and on.'
> [Moy] 'Yes it can, if you just *don't do things.*'
> Sefton said, 'Being human, we are already sinners, we aren't innocent, no one is because of the Fall, because of Original Sin.'
> 'The Fall is ahead,' said Moy, 'and I am afraid of it. How can evil and badness begin in a life, how can it *happen*?' (*GK*, p. 18)

By the end of the novel the Fall is still ahead for Moy but we know it is approaching; she has lost her mystic powers which had earlier made the stones in her room move, her fey powers have faded and she is suffering the agonies of unrequited love. Yet Moy, we believe, unlike Charles in *The Sea, The Sea*, comes out on the other side of innocence into goodness.

By far the most significant discussion of Good and Evil in the novel, however, centres on Peter Mir's death and resurrection. How does he become involved in the original act of aggression, the intention of Lucas to kill his brother Clement? The first version of the story, that put about by Lucas and Clement, and that which everyone believes at the time, is told to us by the narrator; the true version emerges later. Murdoch sets the details of the scene with

care: it is past midnight on a summer evening; Lucas gets Clement
completely drunk before taking him in the car to a remote place
amongst trees and construction rubble with the pretence of showing
him something but with the intention of striking him on the head
with a baseball bat and killing him. As the murder weapon begins
to descend Clement senses it and tries to spring away, observing as
he does so 'the figure beside Lucas of another man' (*GK*, p. 85).
The theatricality of the scene is only equalled by its religious im-
plications: the mysterious third figure manifests himself at the crucial moment and saves Clement's life at the apparent expense of
his own; when Lucas returns from his self-imposed exile he explains, 'one man can die for another' and Clement asks, 'So he
died for me?' (*GK*, p. 91); a little later, as they continue to talk,
Lucas comments 'An angel might have stayed my hand' (*GK*, p. 92).
Immediately after this conversation we are introduced to the figure
of Peter Mir – revived, resurrected, or perhaps an avenging angel
from the beginning: 'An angel', Peter explains to Bellamy, 'is a
messenger of the divine, a messenger is an instrument, sometimes
an unconscious one' (*GK*, p. 299); though he was at the time apply-
ing the words to Lucas, we are able to conceive of Peter himself as
some sort of mystic messenger, an instrument of justice.

In *A Fairly Honourable Defeat* the demonic figure of Julius King
is responsible for Rupert Foster's death but is able to shrug it off,
appearing to feel no guilt and no responsibility for his actions. Before the return of Peter Mir it looks as though this will be exactly
the stance of Lucas Graffe; he has invented a story to tell to the
world, he has involved Clement in his machinations and he appears
to feel no remorse. When Peter appears, however, he demands justice, thought it is soon apparent that it is not legal but moral justice
that he is seeking. He rehearses what justice must demand, 'the
idea of retribution is everywhere fundamental to justice', so that
Lucas's 'just punishment would seem to be . . . a blow upon the
head delivered with equal force' (*GK*, p. 126), in other words the
Old Testament justice of 'an eye for an eye'; more germane to Peter's sense of justice, however, is his desire that Lucas should acknowledge his sin and confess the truth to his friends, the implication
behind this demand being that truth is greater than mere justice.
Lucas's sin is not only against Peter but also against Clement; furthermore, he has trapped Clement into compounding the sin, for

Clement, who is normally decent and truthful, essentially good, has become embroiled in his brother's evil.

On several occasions Bellamy describes Lucas as 'anti-Christ' but he nevertheless loves him. We have seen in earlier novels, particularly in *The Time of the Angels*, how the evil can attract and inspire love and Lucas is certainly loved by a number of the characters in this story. We feel, nevertheless, that the love accorded to Lucas is not sufficient to bring about his salvation; thus the resolution of the plot seems difficult to understand, for Peter, resurrected a second time, recognises that his feelings of hatred and vengeance are more harmful to himself than to Lucas, metes out symbolic justice and makes peace. Lucas, on the other hand, appears to take the reconciliation cynically; even the symbolic retribution of the small slit between his ribs is inflicted not to bring Lucas to a sense of moral right but in order to complete Peter's healing. We might observe that the two stories – that of Gawain and that of Christian redemption are again brought together here; the symbolic retributive wound is a significant aspect of justice in the Gawain legend whilst the wound given to Lucas is, like that of Christ in the Crucifixion, in the side, a connection made for us by Lucas himself when he equates Clement with doubting Thomas. When Clement asks whether the event was about forgiveness, Lucas concurs with the suggestion and ends up with the outrageously smug act of forgiving Clement for 'all the suffering you caused me when we were children' (*GK*, p. 322). It would appear that he, like Julius King, has learned nothing and his piece of the story ends with him taking Aleph from her family and, again like Julius, leaving the country.

The last short section of the novel is entitled 'They Reach the Sea'. For Murdoch the sea is both attractive and awe-inspiring; here it signifies the end of all the journeys, all the quests and we can perhaps see the regenerate characters as 'finding god in their own souls'. Sefton and Harvey are ecstatically happy together in Florence. By the sea, the last acts of the play are played out: Moy emerges from her dark night of the soul and from a near-death experience into a revitalised anticipation of the future; Bellamy, in saving Moy, finds his life transformed; only over the lives of Louise and Clement a question-mark hangs. Through musing about Peter, Louise expresses the sorrows of Christianity:

'how can we ever be happy now? Peter didn't die *for* anything, he died accidentally, senselessly – he appeared out of a mystery which I have never understood, and now he has vanished leaving all *this* behind . . .' (*GK*, p. 454).

Clement, on the other hand, strives to see the point of it all and finally expresses the joys of Christianity: 'And so . . . we betray him, we explain him away, we do not want to think about him or puzzle about him or try to make out what he was in himself . . .' But then follows the triumphant acceptance of belief, 'Peter saved my life, he gave his own life for mine' (*GK*, p. 456). It is a concept that he repeats frequently to himself; he does not see Peter as an instant saviour of them all but he finds him as a god in his own soul.

The Green Knight is highly theatrical, though the technical ingenuities which peppered the earlier novels are largely absent, the most obvious being simply the butcher's knife hidden in Peter Mir's presentation umbrella. Like the narrator of *The Sea, The Sea*, Clement is an actor, though a very much less successful one, and one who has allowed his private life to take precedence over his public role. Actors have frequently trod the boards, and plays and theatre played significant parts, in Murdoch's novels. The reunion between Clement and Louise which takes place in the '*bijou*' theatre south of the river should remind us that their first meeting had taken place in an empty theatre when Teddy Anderson had brought her along to meet Clement; it may also recall for us the reunion (albeit temporary in their case) between Jake and Anna in the little Mime Theatre in Hammersmith Mall in *Under the Net*.

As we have observed, however, what has been most striking throughout the novels, has been the way in which Murdoch uses 'spectacle' to enhance her plots. This partly explains her tacit refusal to abandon the pre-modernist tradition of descriptive detail; we are required to see characters, places, actions as she has envisaged them. We are also frequently put in the remarkable position of viewing incidents as well as experiencing them. In *The Green Knight* there are numerous dramatic incidents, from Harvey's accident on the bridge early in the novel to Bellamy's rescue of Moy from the sea almost at the end. Harvey's two exploits on the Italian bridge are presented to the reader in quite different ways; in the first account we walk the bridge with Harvey himself, part of the action, feeling both his fear and his elation; we see the second walk at the end of the novel through Sefton's eyes and, as spectators, experience vicariously her dread, observing her and observing Harvey only through her fear.

The event which is treated most theatrically, however, is the reenactment of the murder scene. From the first Peter has seen it as 'a sort of rite of purification – a sort of mystery play' (*GK*, p. 250) and, following this, Clement has decided to make it into some sort of histrionic performance. He is convinced of the necessity of this after, returning to the original scene, he sees in his mind's eye, in slow motion and in all its horror, what happened in the original incident and envisages what might have happened. The scene he views is his own near-death and what he clearly at that moment believes was the actual death of Peter Mir. He fears that the reenactment of the scene might bring about a repetition of the violence and perhaps another death for Peter; he thus decides that he must be the director of the play that is to be acted out in order to prevent a recurrence of the original incident. Yet the action is taken out of his hands as we view Peter, bathed in burning light before he falls to the ground like Saul on the road to Damascus; unlike Saul, he is not struck blind but, as in the biblical story, those around him are speechless, unsure of what has happened and they have to take him home. Like Saul, however, Peter has undergone a conversion, the avenging spirit of the Old Testament has left him; he remembers God, as he explains to Bellamy, though it is his Buddhist beliefs he recalls and the Buddha in the soul.

The problem with this novel is that the reader's retrospections and expectations are constantly changing and the theatricality of many of the events does not dispel our unease: if Peter had, indeed recovered from Lucas's blow, is it possible that Lucas would not have been informed? Moreover, we are told quite unequivocally that 'the "assailant" had died without regaining consciousness' (*GK*, p. 88); in this case Lucas would surely have been tried for manslaughter, if not for murder. We are then left with the belief that Peter Mir is a mystical figure, the 'third' who walked beside the two brothers and saved Clement's life and who then became an avenging angel. The difficulty with this interpretation is the conversion of the avenging angel into an angel of mercy, his seizing by Dr Fonsett and his later reported death. Why do Bellamy and the others not go to the

Nursing Home to see Dr Fonsett and ask to attend the funeral? To argue in such a way suggests, I believe, a failure of imagination. The answers to such questions lie in the supernatural and fairy-tale element of the story. Life and death are mysteries; we cannot account for them; the various myths, legends and fairy tales embedded in *The Green Knight* are, as Clement reflects, 'somehow jumbled up and all the wrong way round' (*GK*, p. 431). The not-completely-Green Knight, the inchoate Christ-figure, the fey Moy with her Rapunzel pigtail, the evil magician Lucas, the failed Holy Man Bellamy are pieces of separate jigsaw puzzles which have all been thrown together; they may never come together as a rational whole but they recreate pictures in our minds, fed by our varying stores of knowledge and imagination.

The Green Knight with its mysticism, its interest in religion, its philosophical viewpoints is a far cry from the first novel *Under The Net*. Both novels, however, appear at first to illustrate Murdoch's belief in contingency. We have seen in Chapter 2 above how Jake's trust in 'a sufficient reason' for everything (*UTN*, p. 24) was undermined by events. Here, in the most recent novel, we are aware once more of the way in which chance seems to rule our lives. The encounter which was intended to lead to the death of Clement was interrupted by the chance appearance of Peter, as he explains:

> 'How was it that you and I met on that dark summer night? You of course were there with intent, I as the most accidental of strollers. A minute either way and we would never have met' (*GK*, p. 314).

Thus Lucas's carefully laid plans are frustrated. In the second encounter Clement plans everything in detail once again, and once again the plans are frustrated. Yet, in this later novel there is a strong suggestion that the events as they happened were not left to chance, that it was a mystical but predestined intervention that saved Clement's life, that it was a single incident in a titanic contest between two magicians, the Good and the Evil, between, perhaps, God and Satan. If so, Evil is certainly not vanquished for Lucas lives to accept jauntily his token punishment and to move on to his next evil deed, the abduction of Aleph and the destruction of trust between members of the Anderson family. Like Julius King, like Milton's Satan, like those tied to the Buddhist Wheel, he moves on to another sphere of activity.

The interest in theatre is, as we have seen in all the novels, a continuing one, but in the course of time it seems to me that it has become less spontaneous and more of a structural device. Actors and actresses, theatres and plays dominate the novels almost as often as do writers and books, confirming Murdoch's strong interest in the theatre, particularly in the works of Shakespeare. The looking-in on little theatrical scenes which is so much a part of the actual writing of the earlier novels (see particularly the discussion of *The Bell,* pp. 29f above) has gradually given way to more deliberate dramatic structuring. There are several occasions in *The Green Knight* when most of the characters are brought together in one place, a device of increasing interest to Murdoch because of its dramatic potential. The first of these, a gathering of the Andersons and Blackets and their friends, is staged in order to introduce them to Peter Mir; it is at this introductory meeting that Peter Mir invents his role of psychoanalyst, a role in which both the reader and the other characters in the drama believe until the final grand dinner party in Peter's house. The next such gathering is the masked party to celebrate Moy's sixteenth birthday; because it is a masked party, all the participants assign themselves roles. Peter assumes that of a bull and Moy that of the wise owl who leads the bull into the celebrations; the mythological connections with Zeus who changed into a bull in order to seduce the maiden Europa and with Minerva the wise (whose symbol is an owl), who was born out of Zeus's head are both there and not there; like the mediaeval legend, they are 'all mixed up', thus avoiding a glib symbolic interpretation and simultaneously awakening our imaginations. We might also remember that the owl is a symbol of desolation in the Bible,[1] and of the three girls Moy (certainly at this point in the story) is the saddest and loneliest. The third gathering, which encompasses the *dénouement,* is the party at Peter's house which has been discussed briefly above.

Furthermore, not only have actors such as Charles Arrowby or Clement Graffe become major characters in the novels but also discussion of the role of 'acting', the conscious or subconscious substitution of – or perhaps interplay between – imagination and reality have become dominant. Clement, the actor, sees the whole plot of *The Green Knight* in terms of some sort of play 'the slow enactment

of an awful pantomime' (*GK*, p. 329). The book is divided into
five sections like the five acts of a play; Clement identifies the
various 'Acts' as the three 'events': the original assault on Peter,
its replay, and 'Act Three' – the infliction of symbolic justice (see
GK, p. 329), belonging respectively to sections 1–3 of the novel. On
the other hand, he thinks that Peter's party is to be Act Four, but the
fact that it occurs in section 3 suggests that the real Act Four recounts the death of Peter Mir and the various engagements that take
place in section 4, whilst in section 5, the final Act or the Resolution, they reach the sea (*GK*, p. 451). Thus, we can see the whole
novel as consciously using the framework of a Shakespearean drama.

The ethical and philosophic content of the novels has also changed
and grown over the years. *Under the Net* posited a comparatively
straightforward moral problem, which was not much complicated
by the introduction of a religious dimension in *The Bell*. Later novels,
however, enter into philosophic discussion about the nature of Good
and Evil, about the existence or non-existence of God, about the
relation of morality to religion and about mystic beliefs such as
Buddhism, Judaism or, indeed, Christianity itself. Most people shift
their religious and political perspectives as they grow older, responding to their own explorations and investigations. Murdoch is
no exception and perhaps more than most people she has pursued
trains of thought that have led her through many philosophic and
moral mazes. Her present position as 'Christian fellow-traveller (see
above, p. 11) would seem to represent the religious stance she takes
in *The Green Knight*, where Christian morality prevails without God;
at the same time, she has not shut the door on the imaginative
possibilities of mystic and supernatural belief.

The most striking change in the course of the novels is, I think,
that of atmosphere and tone, yet it is difficult to pin down. All the
novels have their light moments and some, such as *A Severed Head*,
may be seen as almost pure comedy, but, particularly in the later
novels, there is a kind of moral seriousness which is not apparent
even in novels such as *The Bell* or *The Unicorn*. The plots of the
novels are just as gripping, exciting and unpredictable but the reader,
whilst still reading for the story is being forced to consider philosophical and moral concepts. Rather than being given answers, we
are offered questions which stimulate our minds and send us back
to reread the novels, long as they are, again and again.

8
Conclusion

It is perhaps not surprising that a major novelist who has written twenty-five novels over a span of forty years has not always won critical approval and Iris Murdoch's reputation has certainly see-sawed since the publication of her first novel in 1954. One problem is that she defies classification: she is not a Modernist; she is not a Post-Modernist; she is not, like many of her female contemporaries, a feminist writer; yet, despite the fact that she employs many Victorian devices in her novels, no serious reader of her fiction could place her among the traditionalists. She is a thinker, a novelist of ideas, a philosopher who dares to introduce philosophic discussion into her novels; at the same time she is a myth-maker, a weaver of stories, interested in patterns, interested in form, interested above all in establishing a *raison d'être* for truth, goodness and love in a world that has dispensed with God.

Murdoch makes few concessions to the frantic lifestyle of the modern world; her novels get longer and longer; her descriptions continue to be given in minute detail; a full understanding of her fiction demands the learning and culture of Renaissance Man – a knowledge of literature, philosophy, classics, fairy stories and legend, history, psychology, languages, art, drama, music, popular science and probably a dozen other subjects. On the other hand, particularly her earlier novels up to *Henry and Cato*, can be read and appreciated on a completely different level of understanding. She is an excellent storyteller; her novels are full of excitement and anticipation; most of her characters can be accepted on a level realistic enough to satisfy the reader reading for pleasure; there is great ingenuity shown in the planning and execution of all sorts of coups; there is romance for those who want romance, mystery for those who want mystery and there are happiness and humour, genuine comedy of a very high order.

She has chosen throughout her career to write novels about social life, principally the life of the middle and upper middle classes, rather than about the domesticities of family life, and this has brought her criticism on two fronts: first from the feminists, that as a woman, she has not attempted to deal with the problems of modern women and secondly that, though she is writing about late twentieth-century modern life, few of her characters seem to work for their living. Both comments are true or partly true but, as serious criticism, must be seen to be spurious. Murdoch is not writing nineteenth-century industrial novels or twentieth-century feminist novels and her work must not be judged for being different from what the critics would like it to be.

A genuine problem seems to be the occasional failure to integrate the elements of myth and realism, a failure that I think was more pronounced in the earlier books. A particular example is *The Sandcastle* where what seemed to be a realistic story of a failing marriage introduces the mythical Lawrentian figure of the gipsy and leaves us to puzzle about the magic rites of Felicity who is presented at first as a perfectly ordinary girl. We can contrast the presentation of Felicity with that of Moy in *The Green Knight*, where the duality of myth and realism are with us from the outset and Moy is not only one of Louise's children but is also the youngest princess of fairy story; indeed, she is first introduced to us through Joan Blacket's fairy-tale opening.

I have already commented on Murdoch's propensity to tie up all the loose ends at the close of the novels (see p. 32 above) and she herself is aware that this can sometimes appear clumsy. It is at its least effective when the final summarising of events is an integral part of the plot, has significant bearing on it and yet appears as a mere appendage, as in *The Red and the Green*. Such minor problems, however, are insignificant, set against the vast achievement of the whole body of the novels.

Almost from the beginning of her career as author she has attracted conflicting criticism. When *Under the Net* first appeared its author was not quite unknown, for her book on Sartre had been published the year before. Sartre's place in the philosophic and literary world was by then firmly established as a novelist, as a dramatist and as the principal proponent of existentialism; his famous work on existentialism, *L'être et le néant* (*Being and Nothingness*) (1943), was not translated into English until 1956, so Murdoch's book would have been seen by many literary critics as a way into some sort of understanding of Sartre's philosophy and thus of his literary outlook. Hence, her name and her academic interests would already be known.

For a first novel *Under the Net* was given very fair treatment, being widely reviewed and in general looked upon favourably. The reviewer in *The Times Literary Supplement* for 9 July 1954 was especially enthusiastic, commenting that 'Miss Murdoch has wit, intelligence and sympathy. She can create character; she has a light hand with dialogue'; weaknesses were recognised but were seen to 'pale into their proper significance'. It is the review in the 'Arts section' of *The Times* on 5 June 1954, however that seems to me particularly perceptive and prophetic. *Under the Net* was reviewed together with Conrad Richter's *The Light in the Forest*; the two books were reviewed briefly, though Murdoch was accorded about six column inches, nearly three times the amount of space given to Richter. What impresses one most in hindsight is the way in which the reviewer perceived Murdoch's vision of life. 'Life to her', he remarked, 'would seem to be a vast, darkened room with at the farther end a chink of light under the door to which naturally ... you make your way' (*The Times*, 5 June 1954). This Platonic image, itself a metaphor for Plato's cave, has, as we have seen, become one of the most significant of all Murdoch's images in the novels that have followed.

The other three early novels were all given favourable treatment in *The Times Literary Supplement*. On the publication of *The Bell* Murdoch was accorded an almost full-page review on 7 November 1958 which surveyed all her fiction up to that time. The novels were sensitively handled; the idea that Murdoch belonged to the 'Angry' brigade was rejected and she was particularly praised for her handling of male characters. There was too, a recognition of the intellectual quality of her work:

the conjunction of a brilliant imagination and a passionate concern for conveying moral concepts is so rare among young contemporary novelists that Miss Murdoch refuses to fit into the usual critical judgment of fiction.

Such a thoughtful and perceptive review article would seem to have been a positive affirmation of Murdoch's position among the leading novelists of the day.

The Times reviews, however, were not so well-disposed. *The Flight from the Enchanter* and *The Sandcastle* were reviewed respectively on 29 March 1956 and 9 May 1957, each together with four other novels, both briefly, and both with what I detect as an air of condescension towards women novelists. *The Bell* (6 November 1958) fared better, though the reviewer considered that it 'goes on for a little too long'; I wonder what he makes of the more recent novels?

The novels which I have grouped together in Chapter 3 really began the carping criticism that has persisted to dog Murdoch's fiction. Yet the critics were curiously at odds with each other;[1] her language and prose style are praised or criticised at various times and by various reviewers, though the same novels are being discussed: for instance, she has 'little natural talent for the writing of fiction' and she 'is a marvellous storyteller'. Reading back over these early reviews now, one has the definite impression that the writers often did not understand the novel being reviewed and, in fact, the reviewer of *The Unicorn* in *The Times* (5 September 1963) confesses as much, though he is generous in his praise.

The reviewer's job, particularly in daily or weekly papers, is always a difficult one: the book has to be read (sometimes together with three or four other books) conclusions come to and a review of a specified length produced in what can be a very short space of time. It is little wonder that novels as complicated as Murdoch's are often not fully absorbed.

In 1965 the first full-length book on Murdoch's work appeared. *Degrees of Freedom* by fellow-novelist A. S. Byatt discusses the first seven novels sensitively, perceptively and knowledgeably.[2] Byatt herself may be seen as a sharp contrast to Murdoch in that she works slowly and has a very slender output; by 1965 the only novel she had published was *The Shadow of the Sun* (1964), though the next novel *The Game* was already in gestation. In the introduction to a later edition of *The Shadow of the Sun* (1991) Byatt pays a personal tribute to Murdoch, coupling her with Proust and commenting that they both 'combine a kind of toughness of thought with a sensuous awareness that is part of their thought',[3] and implying that this reading was valuable to her when she wrote the final draft of the novel.

Degrees of Freedom did much to help enhance Murdoch's reputation, for not only is it a very balanced assessment of the early novels but it also enables us to put into perspective the relationship between Murdoch's early fiction and her philosophic thought. Byatt puts her finger on the problems faced by reviewers when she explains in her final chapter why she wrote the book:

> [Murdoch's novels] presented themselves . . . like puzzles out of which a plan of ideas, a scheme of references could be extracted for examination, *with some effort*. That effort was required *could . . .* be seen as a criticism of Miss Murdoch as a novelist, depending on whether the complication and occasional obscurity of her presentation of her thought is to be seen as necessary or simply irritatingly baffling. . . . to make the effort to understand her thought, to find the statement of the abstract ideas behind her novels is in a sense the best way to come at these, and ultimately to make a critical judgment of them [my italics] (*DOF*, p. 181).

A genuine and balanced response to Murdoch's novels, Byatt suggests, demands effort and intensive thought if one is to savour anything like their full flavour. It is clear that Byatt admires Murdoch's work but she is by no means a blind idolator and she is thus able to suggest what she sees as shortcomings in the novels without allowing her criticisms to be destructive. Her main problems are associated with word-usage – the occasional use of a vague rhetorical style, indulgence in clichés, 'large passages of . . . unsuccessful long rhetoric and philosophical shorthand' (*DOF*, p. 214). The book concludes, however, with the view that any criticism must be offset by the good qualities and in the belief that Murdoch's 'gifts are various and considerable; what she will make of them finally we cannot prophesy, but from what she has done already it is clear that it is of importance to us' (*DOF*, p. 216).

The significance of this book coming at the time it did was that it acted as an antidote to the adverse criticism that was beginning to appear both in the press and in academic journals and perhaps did something to persuade reviewers and critics that a hasty assessment of the novels was an impossibility. Thus, though its scope was limited as it was able to encompass only seven of the novels, this was perhaps the most influential book on Murdoch ever to have been written. Just over ten years later, in 1976, Byatt published a pamphlet on Murdoch for the British Council. Of necessity much shorter than *Degrees of Freedom*, it does not add a great deal to the general points made in the longer book, though it discusses more fully some of the philosophical aspects of Murdoch's thought.

From the mid-1960s onward an academic industry has grown up around Murdoch; it has produced innumerable articles, a fair number of theses and her books have been set as undergraduate texts. Especially notable, perhaps, was the 'Special Number' of *Modern Fiction Studies* dedicated to her work in Autumn 1969 (vol. XV, no. 63), not so much because of the quality of the articles in it but in view of the fact that most special numbers up to that time were concerned with authors already dead (Graham Greene, J. D. Salinger and Lawrence Durrell were also exceptions). It thus placed Murdoch among the serious contemporary novelists at a significant central point in her career.

Not only critical but also public recognition has been gradually accorded Murdoch (see above, p. 7). It began in 1973 when she was awarded the James Tait Black Memorial Prize for *The Black Prince*. When she received the Whitbread Literary Award for Fiction in the following year for *The Sacred and Profane Love Machine* C. P. Snow, who presented her with the award, commented that though *The Sacred and Profane Love Machine* was 'not perhaps her best novel', the judges 'wished to acknowledge her achievement as a major contemporary British novelist' (see *The Times*, 19 April 1974, p. 17). The Whitbread Committee was probably regretting that they had neglected to mark the publication of *The Black Prince*, which was considered by many, if not most, critics at the time to be her best novel to date. In 1978 *The Sea, The Sea* was awarded the Booker Prize and two of her other novels – *The Good Apprentice* (1985) and *The Book and the Brotherhood* (1987) have since been nominated for it.

Together with her husband, John Bayley, Iris Murdoch has frequently been invited to give talks or to speak at conferences and she has given many interviews. She is always generous with her time and seems to enjoy talking about her own novels, her philosophical ideas and literature in general.

It seems inevitable that such a prolific novelist will have both her admirers and her detractors. Thoughtful adverse criticism based on a fair reading of the novels and fully documented must be considered seriously but it is often disturbing to find that the detractors have made very little effort to try to understand the novels. It has recently become a sort of public game to make brief mention of Murdoch and her novels in interviews or other ephemeral writings. So Miles Kington in *The Independent* for 27 October 1993 makes slighting references to the whole body of her novels except for *Under the Net* which he apparently enjoyed reading; he goes on to mention that 'two well-known writers' of his own age agreed with his criticism and then makes the revealing comments that one of them had never finished a novel by Murdoch and that the other had never read one at all. Denis Healey, too, after describing Murdoch as 'a friend of mine as a student', appears to consider *A Severed Head* as her best novel and confesses that he has not tried to read the later novels (*The Observer Magazine*, 6 March 1994). These are basically trivial comments but they appear in national papers and are widely read. Perhaps we can see them as being offset by a similarly trivial but nevertheless very public acclamation of the interest of her work when we sit in the tube train and observe that British Rail in one of its advertisements shows us a passenger sitting comfortably, reading a Penguin copy of Iris Murdoch. Both these kinds of public comment appear to suggest that Murdoch is part of the contemporary scene, that her name is well-known even outside academic circles and that her books are read, or at least talked about by a wide variety of people.

Notes

Chapter 1

1. The Bibliography lists all Iris Murdoch's books and gives dates of first publication and full information of editions cited. References are given in the text under short titles which are listed in the Bibliography and in 'Abbreviations' at the front of the book.
2. J.-L. Chevalier (ed.) *Rencontres avec Iris Murdoch*, Caen: Centre de Recherches de Littérature et Linguistique, l'Université de Caen, 1978, p. 93. References hereafter will be to *Rencontres*.
3. John Haffenden, *Novelists in Interview*, London: Methuen & Co. Ltd, 1985, p. 201. References hereafter will be to Haffenden.
4. *The Times*, 27 August 1975, p. 11.
5. First published in *Encounter*, January 1961; reprinted in Malcolm Bradbury (ed.) *The Novel Today*, Glasgow: Fontana/Collins, 1977, pp. 23–31. References hereafter will be to Bradbury.
6. Reynolds Stone (1909–79), well-known as designer and engraver, was Murdoch's friend for many years. In 1970 she dedicated *A Fairly Honourable Defeat* to him and his wife Janet.

Chapter 2

1. One of a series of pamphlets on 'Contemporary Writers' published in conjunction with the British Council, 1988.
2. See, for instance, *The Unicorn*, *The Italian Girl*, *The Time of the Angels*.
3. A. S. Byatt, *Degrees of Freedom*, London: Chatto & Windus, 1965, p. 73. References hereafter will be to *DOF*.

Chapter 3

1. A. S. Byatt, *Iris Murdoch*, London: Longman; published for the British Council, 1976, p. 26.
2. Leonard Kriegel, 'Iris Murdoch: Everybody through the Looking Glass' in Charles Shapiro (ed.) *Contemporary British Novelists*, Carbondale: South Illinois University Press, 1965, p. 73.

Chapter 4

1. Originally published in *The Anatomy of Knowledge*, 1969, this essay was republished in Iris Murdoch, *The Sovereignty of Good*, London: Routledge & Kegan Paul, 1970. Edition cited: Penguin Books (PB) reprint, 1974. References hereafter will be to *SOG*.
2. Originally delivered as the Leslie Stephen Lecture in 1967. Published in *The Sovereignty of Good* (see above, note 1). References hereafter will be to *SOG*.
3. Quoted from William Blake, 'Introduction' in *Songs of Innocence*.
4. Iris Murdoch, *The Fire and the Sun*, Oxford: Clarendon Press, 1977, p. 4.

Chapter 5

1. Peter Conradi, *Iris Murdoch; The Saint and the Artist*, 2nd edn, Basingstoke: Macmillan, 1989, pp. 195f.
2. Deborah Johnson, *Iris Murdoch*, Brighton: The Harvester Press, 1987, p. 36.

Chapter 6

1. See *The Sea, The Sea,* p. 39; and *The Tempest* V.1.50–7.

Chapter 7

1. See, for instance, Psalm 102.6, 'I am like a pelican of the wilderness: I am like an owl of the desert.'

Chapter 8

1. See, for instance, reviews in *The Times Literary Supplement* for: 6 September 1963, 10 September 1964, 14 October 1965, 8 September 1966, 25 June 1968 and *The Times* for: 15 June 1961, 7 June 1962, 10 September 1964, 14 October 1965, 8 September 1966, 27 January 1968.
2. A. S. Byatt, *Degrees of Freedom*, London: Chatto & Windus, 1965.
3. A. S. Byatt, *The Shadow of the Sun*, London: Vintage Edition, 1991, p. xii.

Select Bibliography

Works by Iris Murdoch

Novels

All the novels were originally published by Chatto & Windus, London. References in the text cite the reprints published by Penguin Books (PB), Harmondsworth, Middlesex, except for *The Sacred and Profane Love Machine*, *A Word Child*, *Henry and Cato* and *The Green Knight* where the first edition is cited; for all other novels the date in brackets refers to first publication and the second date to the edition cited.

Under the Net (1954); 1960 (Cited in references as *UNT*)
The Flight from the Enchanter (1956); 1962 (Cited in references as *FE*)
The Sandcastle (1957); 1987 (Cited in references as *TS*)
The Bell (1958); 1967
A Severed Head (1961); 1964 (Cited in references as *ASH*)
An Unofficial Rose (1962); 1966 (Cited in references as *AUR*)
The Unicorn (1963); 1967 (Cited in references as *TU*)
The Italian Girl (1964); 1967 (Cited in references as *TIG*)
The Red and the Green (1965); 1967 (Cited in references as *TRATG*)
The Time of the Angels (1966); 1969 (Cited in references as *TOA*)
The Nice and the Good (1968); 1969 (Cited in references as *TNTG*)
Bruno's Dream (1969); 1970 (Cited in references as *BD*)
A Fairly Honourable Defeat (1970); 1980 (Cited in references as *FHD*)
An Accidental Man (1971); 1973
The Black Prince (1973); 1975 (Cited in references as *BP*)
The Sacred and Profane Love Machine (1974)
A Word Child (1975)

Henry and Cato (1976) (Cited in references as *HC*)
The Sea, The Sea (1978); 1980 (Cited in references as *The Sea*)
Nuns and Soldiers (1980); 1982 (Cited in references as *NS*)
The Philosopher's Pupil (1983); 1984 (Cited in references as *PP*)
The Good Apprentice (1985); 1986 (Cited in references as *GA*)
The Book and the Brotherhood (1987); 1988
The Message to the Planet (1989); 1990 (Cited in references as *MTTP*)
The Green Knight (1994) (Cited in references as *GK*)

Other works

Where two dates are given the second refers to edition cited in text.

Sartre: Romantic Rationalist (1953) Harmondsworth: Penguin Books, 1989
    (Cited in references as *SRR*)
'Against Dryness' (1961) in *Encounter*, XVI (January 1961) pp. 16–20;
    reprinted in Malcolm Bradbury (ed.) Glasgow: Fontana/Collins, 1977,
    pp. 23–31 (Cited in references as Bradbury)
The Sovereignty of Good, London: Routledge & Kegan Paul (1970), 1974
    (Cited in references as *SOG*)
The Fire and the Sun, Oxford: Clarendon Press (1977) (Cited in refer-
    ences as *FAS*)
A Year of Birds (1978); London: Chatto & Windus, 1984
The Three Arrows and The Servants and the Snow, 1973; London: Chatto
    & Windus/Hogarth Press, 1985
Acastos (1986), Harmondsworth: Penguin Books, 1987
Metaphysics as a Guide to Morals, London: Chatto & Windus, 1992 (Cited
    in references as *MGM*)

Works Referred to in the Text

Bayley, John, *The Characters of Love*, London: Constable, 1960
Byatt, A. S., *The Shadow of the Sun*, London: Vintage Books, 1991
Byatt, A. S., *Degrees of Freedom*, London: Chatto & Windus, 1965 (Cited
    in references as *DOF*)
Byatt, A. S., *Iris Murdoch*, Harlow: Longman Group Ltd (for The British
    Council), 1976
Byatt, A. S., 'Contemporary Writers: Iris Murdoch', Book Trust Pamphlet
    published in conjunction with the British Council, 1988
Chevalier, J.-L. (ed.) *Rencontres avec Iris Murdoch*, Centre de Recherches
    de Littérature et Linguistique des Pays de Langue Anglaise, l'Université

de Caen, 1978 (Cited in references as *Rencontres*)

Conradi, Peter, *Iris Murdoch: The Saint and the Artist*, Basingstoke: Macmillan (1986); 2nd edn, 1989

Dipple, Elizabeth, *Iris Murdoch: Work for the Spirit*, London: Methuen, 1982

Haffenden, John, *Novelists in Interview*, London: Methuen, 1985 pp. 191–209 (Cited in references as Haffenden)

Johnson, Deborah, *Iris Murdoch*, Brighton: The Harvester Press, 1987

Kriegel, Leonard, 'Iris Murdoch: Everybody through the Looking Glass' in Charles Shapiro (ed.) *Contemporary British Novelists*, Carbondale: South Illinois University Press, 1965

Modern Fiction Studies (Special Number), XV, 3, 1969

The Times

The Times Literary Supplement

Index

'Angry' Movement, 24, 123

Bayley, John, 6–7, 9, 16, 126
Beckett, Samuel, 34
Blake, William, 57, 59, 130n
Brooke, Rupert, 46
Buddha, *see* Religious ideas
Byatt, A. S., 32, 44, 124–6, 129n,
    130n, 131n

Carroll, Lewis, 3, 45, 130n
Classical mythology, 43, 44, 76,
    77, 81, 110, 119
Conrad, Joseph, 92
Conradi, Peter, 76, 130n

Deconstruction, 23, 54, 74, 78
Derrida, Jacques, 108
Drama, use of, 13, 16, 19–20, 21,
    22–3, 24, 26, 28, 29–30, 32,
    33, 34, 40, 41, 42, 45, 47,
    48–9, 62, 63, 69, 73, 78–9,
    86, 92, 93–4, 95, 113–14,
    115, 116–17, 119–20 (*see
    also* Shakespeare)

Eckhart, Meister, 112
Education, 2, 4, 11, 26, 37
Eliot, T. S., 98
Evil, *see* Religious ideas

Faustus, 58
Feminism, 2–3, 121, 122

Freud, Sigmund, 79

Gawain and the Green Knight,
    110–11, 115, 118, 119
God, *see* Religious ideas
Golding, William, 55, 87
Good, *see* Religious ideas
Gothic aspects, 47, 48, 56, 74

Haffenden, John, 2, 12, 16, 56,
    129n

James, Henry, 14–15
Johnson, Deborah, 78, 130n
Joyce, James, 109

Kafka, Franz, 16–17
Kant, Immanuel, 9, 55–6, 70

'Lady of Shalott, The', 48, 49
Le Gros, Bernard, 7, 8
Listener, The, 8
Lolita, 81

Mathias, William, 11
Milton, John, 96, 113, 118
Modern Fiction Studies, 126
Modernism, 1, 121
Morris, William, 103
Murdoch, Iris, Works by
    *Acastos: Two Platonic
        Dialogues*, 10
    Accidental Man, An, 15, 55, 71, 73

137